COURTING A RELUCTANT ALLY

An Evaluation of U.S./UK Naval Intelligence
Cooperation, 1935-1941

LCDR Gregory J. Florence, USN

With a Foreword by
Rear Admiral Thomas A. Brooks, USN (Ret.)
Former Director of Naval Intelligence

The Joint Military Intelligence College supports and encourages research on intelligence issues that distills lessons and improves support to policy-level and operational consumers

As the U.S. Intelligence Community debates how to engage in intelligence cooperation and information sharing with a variety of other countries, in the face of non-state malefactors, we need not remain without a rudder. Lieutenant Commander Florence demonstrates in this book that the question of how to proceed toward useful information sharing and cooperation can be addressed by exploiting our national archives. His research reveals how a contentious, interwar relationship between the U.S. and the UK evolved into a special relationship as information sharing and cooperation in intelligence creation and use became indispensable. This publication highlights the value of historical research carried out by candidates for the degree of Master of Science of Strategic Intelligence.

This document is based exclusively on sources available to the public. The views expressed are those of the author, and do not necessarily reflect the official policy or position of the Department of Defense or the U.S. Government.

This publication has been approved for unrestricted distribution by the Directorate for Freedom of Information and Security Review, Washington Headquarters Service.

Russell.Swenson@dia.mil, Editor

CONTENTS

FOREWORD

To most Americans alive today, the close alliance between the United States and Great Britain seems to be a "natural" thing, perhaps the inevitable expression of what Winston Churchill referred to as the "special relationship" occasioned by "underlying cultural unity." There are now few among us whose memories go back to the period between the two world wars and who would be able to point out that, commonalities of language and culture notwithstanding, today's special relationship between the United States and Great Britain is a quite recent phenomenon, really dating only from the 1940-41 timeframe.

For much of the two and a quarter centuries of our independence, relationships with Great Britain have been cool or even strained. Cooperation and intelligence sharing with the British in World War I was late in coming and limited in scope. At the end of the war, it slowed to an almost imperceptible trickle, and was very slow to resume. The author outlines the factors accounting for the reluctance of both sides to share information and the underlying feeling of competitiveness between the Royal Navy and the U.S. Navy during the interwar years. This had moderated by the outbreak of hostilities in 1939, but within a year two different dynamics had arisen: the American concern after the fall of France that the British might be quickly defeated, and thus US technical and intelligence information compromised; and the British single-minded focus on bringing America into the war and gaining access to our vast technological and industrial resources. To further their goals, the British were willing to provide the United States with virtually unlimited access to British secrets — technological as well as intelligence — even without any quid pro quo. Their strategy worked. The author outlines how the exchange of information started as a trickle, turned into a flood, and endures to this day.

Most books dealing with U.S.-British cooperation during World War II naturally focus on the war in Europe and highlight the great British cryptologic success with the German Enigma codes (actually a Polish-French-British success). Many leave the reader with the impression that the United States, in gaining access to Enigma decrypts and Royal Navy operational intelligence techniques, got the better half of the bargain. But this is far from a complete picture. It was the Americans who broke the Japanese diplomatic codes and gave codes and machines to the British, and the Americans who provided the bulk of the effort and success against JN-25, the Japanese navy operational code, although British, Dutch, and Australian cryptanalysts contributed significantly during the war. American scientists and laboratory-industry efforts significantly upgraded the technology used to break Enigma codes. Also, OPINTEL, as it exists in the U.S.

Navy today, owes as much to the efforts of the Pacific Fleet Combat Intelligence Unit (also known as Fleet Radio Unit Pacific or Station HYPO) as it does to the British Operational Intelligence Centre.

A number of books have been written about this wartime intelligence cooperation, but this work is the first that provides significant detail on the rocky road toward cooperation that both navies traversed through the 1920s and 1930s. The author has tapped a number of original sources and archives which had not previously been plumbed to provide a new perspective on recent, but largely unappreciated naval history. The reader may find himself reflecting that relationships which appear so "natural" today, were not always that way, and recalling the words of Chaim Herzog, who as President of Israel, declared that nations don't have permanent friends or enemies, only "permanent interests."

Thomas A. Brooks
Rear Admiral, United States Navy (ret.)
Former Director of Naval Intelligence

PROLOGUE

Since World War II, the United States and the United Kingdom have mutually benefited from an unprecedented "special relationship" with regard to intelligence sharing and cooperation. What were the origins of that relationship and what lessons can be derived from its development? While it may seem obvious that the common Axis threat drove both countries to increased levels of intelligence sharing, the extent of the cooperation eventually attained would have surprised many on both sides of the Atlantic prior to World War II. Despite a brief period as allies during World War I, the U.S. and the UK quickly reverted to their traditional roles as strategic competitors following the conclusion of the Great War. A highly visible aspect of that competition was in the area of naval forces, in which both countries invested considerable diplomatic, economic, and military resources. Notwithstanding this rivalry, their naval intelligence cooperation during World War II is often cited as one of the most successful in history. How did this "special relationship" develop, given the contentiousness that existed between these two countries in the interwar period? An analysis of this period indicates one significant factor was the aggressive pursuit of naval intelligence cooperation by the British as part of their larger strategy to secure U.S. entry into the war. The tactics the British employed to secure this cooperation are of interest, as history has shown the British were able to overcome significant distrust on the part of American officials, who were extremely wary of British intentions.

Like the UK, the U.S. is interested in developing intelligence cooperation arrangements with states, such as Russia and India, with whom our country has had inimical or competitive relationships.[1] An assessment of the UK's overall strategy for establishing a closer intelligence relationship with the U.S. can yield insights into effective strategies the U.S. could use to enhance intelligence cooperation with countries that have had, or continue to have, competitive relations with the United States. Second, an analysis of this subject is of historical importance to the Intelligence Community (IC) since the intelligence-sharing agreements between the U.S., the UK, and its former dominions had their antecedents in the World War II period and it is important to understand the rationale behind their

---

[1]The White House, "Joint Statement Between U.S. and India," 9 November 2001, *The White House*, URL:<http://www.whitehouse.gov/news/releases/2001/11/20011109-10.html>, accessed 16 November 2003; The White House, "Press Briefing by National Security Advisor Dr. Condoleezza Rice on the President's Trip to Europe and Russia," *The White House*, URL:<http://www.whitehouse.gov/news/ releases/2002/05/20020520-9.html >, accessed 16 November 2003.

development. Third, this was a critical period in defining the components of what would later become the U.S. IC, particularly naval intelligence. The Office of Naval Intelligence (ONI), in addition to engaging in internecine battles with other intelligence organizations, also faced internal Navy disputes over its own roles and functions. Understanding this period is important to understanding the role ONI currently plays in the IC structure.

Chapter 1

THE STATUS OF INTELLIGENCE SYSTEMS IN THE UNITED STATES AND GREAT BRITAIN

Some of these difficulties stemmed directly from technical obstacles which limited the amount and type of intelligence that could be obtained....Those that were mainly organizational in character arose from the various pressures and resistances—administrative, psychological and political—which complicate relations whenever several bodies share responsibility in a single field. They were all the more intractable, however, because developments in the field of intelligence were setting up conflict between the need for new organizational departures and the established, and perfectly understandable, distribution of intelligence responsibilities.

Francis Hally Hinsley and others, *British Intelligence in the Second World War: Its Influence on Strategy and Operations*

Francis Hinsley's comprehensive, official history of British Intelligence during World War II describes the overall state of British intelligence on the eve of the war. Hinsley's comments about British intelligence could have equally been applied to its U.S. counterpart, which was also rife with bureaucratic rivalry and had to cope with new organizational arrangements designed to handle new sources of intelligence. Understanding how each country approached intelligence, and how each managed the organizational structures they developed in the interwar period to collect, analyze, and disseminate it, is fundamental to fathoming the evolution of the intelligence relationship between the U.S. and the UK. Although many authors have denigrated U.S. intelligence capabilities during the interwar years, recent scholarship has shown that, despite its many problems, the U.S. was probably not far behind the other major powers of the time.[2] Resource constraints, the ill-defined nature of the threat, and the lack of strategic direction all contributed to weaknesses in U.S. intelligence of the 1920s and 30s. The Navy's ONI suffered from other difficulties, as well, since it was beset with internecine conflicts within the Navy Department over its role, and also lacked

---

[2] Rhodri Jeffreys-Jones, "The Role of British Intelligence in the Mythologies Underpinning the OSS and Early CIA," in *American-British-Canadian Intelligence Relations 1939-2000*, ed. David Stafford and Rhodri Jeffreys-Jones (Portland, OR: Frank Cass Publishers, 2000), 5-10; Richard J. Aldrich, *Intelligence and the War Against Japan: Britain, America, and the Politics of Secret Service* (Cambridge: Cambridge University Press, 2000), 96-97.

focus in its mission due to the competing requirements of its intelligence and security functions. These weaknesses were familiar to the British. Their understanding of ONI and overall American intelligence deficiencies would factor into the approaches they used to elicit cooperation.

The American Intelligence Architecture

Many authors have documented the weaknesses of U.S. intelligence in the interwar period. First, it was seriously under-resourced. After World War I, the U.S. drew down its military forces considerably and intelligence, never a coveted assignment during peacetime, faced substantial cuts in fiscal and personnel resources.[3] There were the two Service intelligence divisions, the Navy's ONI and the Army's Military Intelligence Division (MID), both of which were responsible for the collection and analysis of military and political information to support war planning and procurement, as well as security and counterintelligence. A third component of the architecture was the State Department's diplomatic corps, which provided political intelligence to support U.S. foreign policy and economic decisionmaking. The final element was the Federal Bureau of Investigation (FBI), which had principal responsibility for domestic counterintelligence and counterespionage, although its mandate ultimately extended to countries in Central and South America as well. For the most part, intelligence was gained from open-source exploitation, diplomatic and attaché reporting, some limited clandestine Human Intelligence (HUMINT) activity, and some Signals Intelligence (SIGINT).[4]

The main problem with the U.S. intelligence system in the interwar period was the lack of coordination between its four component intelligence organizations. There was no central coordinating authority for their efforts, which often led to duplicative collection, analysis, and reporting of information. Bureaucratic turf battles and inter-departmental rivalries were common features of the intelligence landscape, which inhibited cooperation in many cases.[5] In addition to the highly compartmentalized nature of U.S. intelligence, analytic reports were often cited for their lack of rigor or utility. The U.S. also had no real operational intelligence capability at either the Service Headquarters or the national level.[6] British observers of U.S. intelligence noted all these flaws in the U.S. system and also believed that U.S. intelligence was inadequate because it lacked such organizational structures as a Special Operations Executive (SOE) for conducting covert

---

[3] Aldrich, 32.

[4] Aldrich, 95.

[5] Donald MacLachlan, *Room 39: A Study in Naval Intelligence* (New York: Atheneum, 1968), 223-224; Aldrich 95.

[6] Bradley F. Smith, *The Ultra-Magic Deals: And the Most Secret Special Relationship, 1940-1946* (Novato, CA: Presidio Press, 1993), 30-31. Cited hereafter as Smith, *Ultra-Magic Deals*.

action, a propaganda unit, or an economic warfare division — all of which were considered essential by the British for prosecuting a modern war.[7] Finally, there was little impetus on the part of the top decisionmaker in the U.S., Franklin Roosevelt, to adjust the U.S. intelligence organization architecture. Roosevelt, who personally directed the efforts of ONI when he was the Assistant Secretary of the Navy during World War I, understood the value of intelligence but he preferred to receive information from a variety of sources, even if that information proved contradictory. Additionally, he employed his own personal network of agents to obtain information he desired, which added to the fragmentation of U.S. intelligence.[8]

Various decisionmakers within U.S. intelligence saw the problems listed above and there were attempts made to increase collaboration and coordination at various stages throughout the inter-war period. Sharing between the departments did occur, but, more often than not, this was based on personalities of the individuals engaged in the sharing rather than some structural mechanism designed to enhance cooperation. At various periods in the interwar period, ONI did seek closer ties with the other departments but most of these efforts did little to systematically improve coordination.[9] One bright spot was in the area of SIGINT cooperation, where joint work by the Army and the Navy led to successes with the Japanese diplomatic code known as PURPLE. But these efforts were part of the Navy's communications organization, not ONI. Still, there was no cooperation between the two services on the task of breaking the Japanese Service codes. Even the cooperation on the diplomatic codes was colored by service rivalries. A rather convoluted system, whereby the Army and Navy would break and then brief the President on PURPLE decrypts on alternate days, was instituted to ensure both services would receive credit for their work on this highly valuable intelligence source.[10] Although recommendations for how to achieve closer cooperation among the disparate organizations within American intelligence were put

---

[7] Aldrich, 95.

[8] Jeffery M. Dorwart, *Conflict of Duty: The U.S. Navy's Intelligence Dilemma, 1919-1945* (Annapolis, MD: Naval Institute Press, 1983), 164-171, cited hereafter as Dorwart, *Conflict of Duty*; Arthur M. Schlesinger, *The Coming of the New Deal*, vol. 2 of *The Age of Roosevelt* (Boston, MA: Houghton Mifflin Company, 1959), 523; Steve Weiss, *Allies in Conflict: Anglo-American Strategic Negotiations, 1938-44* (New York: St. Martin's Press, Inc., 2001), 29.

[9] Dorwart, *Conflict of Duty*, 69-70.

[10] Roland H. Worth, *Secret Allies in the Pacific: Covert Intelligence and Code Breaking Cooperation Between the United States, Great Britain, and Other Nations Prior to the Attack on Pearl Harbor* (Jefferson, NC: McFarland, 2001), 16-17; Ronald H. Spector, *Listening to the Enemy: Key Documents on the Role of Communications Intelligence in the War with Japan* (Wilmington, DE: Scholarly Resources, Inc., 1988), 8; Aldrich, 73.

forward, some by ONI, no real improvement in this situation occurred until the founding of the Coordinator of Information office, the predecessor to the Office of Strategic Services (OSS), in the summer of 1941.[11] As noted later in this study, the founding of this office did correct some of the deficiencies in the U.S. intelligence system, but overcoming bureaucratic barriers was a difficulty throughout the war period and is an issue the Intelligence Community has continued to wrestle with to the present day.

ONI: Organization and Limitations of America's First Intelligence Service

The organization which would one day become ONI was first formed in 1882 as the Navy realized its need for information in peacetime that would assist in the war-planning and procurement that was required to fight in any future conflict.[12] ONI's responsibilities evolved over time, but by 1938 its principal responsibilities included collection and analysis on foreign countries, particularly on their naval establishments; administration of the naval attaché program; Navy public relations; "operation of the Navy's public records and library; preparation and dissemination of data on our own and foreign navies"; counterespionage; and security.[13] To meet these requirements, ONI was organized into branches to deal with Foreign Intelligence, Domestic Intelligence, Historical Records, and Public Relations.[14] These branches were further subdivided into country desks and offices meant to address specific technical issues, such as gunnery. In terms of regional assessments, ONI focused on Russia, because of the fear of communism and its influence on the workers in industries critical to the Navy, and on Japan, which was seen as the main threat and was the focus of U.S. naval war planning.[15]

As noted earlier, resource constraints were a significant factor limiting the effectiveness of ONI. At the end of World War I, there were 306 officers working in ONI's Washington, DC offices, but by 1935 that number had dwindled to 21

---

[11] Wyman H. Packard, *A Century of Naval Intelligence* (Washington, DC: GPO, 1996), 16, 225; Dorwart, *Conflict of Duty*, 119-120.

[12] Alan Harris Bath, *Tracking the Axis Enemy: The Triumph of Anglo-American Naval Intelligence* (Lawrence, KS: University Press of Kansas, 1998), 4.

[13] Packard, 323.

[14] Parkard, 321-323.

[15] Columbia University, *The Reminiscences of Royal E. Ingersoll* (New York: Oral History Research Office, 1965), 46, Operational Archives, Naval Historical Center, Washington, DC. Cited hereafter as *Ingersoll Reminiscences*.

officers assisted by 20 civilian clerks.[16] Complicating the personnel issue for ONI was the fact that many naval officers saw little value in doing intelligence work. Consequently, there were relatively few intelligence professionals among the naval officer corps since most believed multiple assignments in intelligence would be detrimental to their careers. Even the Director of Naval Intelligence (DNI) position was looked upon with disdain. VADM Kirk, who as RADM Kirk was DNI from January to October 1941, has noted in retrospect that

> [t]he average tour of the Director of Naval Intelligence, in the ten years before we went in the war, was less than two years, always. Nobody was staying. It had very poor standing in the Navy Department, not because of the calibre [sic] of the officers, but everybody sort of thought Naval Intelligence was striped pants, cookie-pushers, [and] going to parties.[17]

VADM Kirk's views were echoed by one of the few officers who did multiple tours in intelligence at that time, Rear Admiral Ellis Zacharias, who felt that the high turnover rate of the DNI's and their relative lack of experience with intelligence matters, were two factors that significantly limited the effectiveness of ONI.[18]

Another major problem ONI had to contend with was the dichotomy between its positive intelligence functions and its security and counterintelligence functions. Lacking the resources to do either job adequately, the effort depended largely on who held the DNI position. Throughout much of the 1920s and 30s, DNIs primarily focused on ONI's security role at the expense of the positive intelligence mission.[19] Undermanned, ONI was forced to use untrained reservists and volunteers to augment the personnel involved with security in the country's various naval districts. While it is true that the Navy faced potentially significant problems from radical elements and labor agitators throughout the 1920s and 30s, much of the workforce involved in the domestic intelligence mission was not trained in proper investigative techniques. This situation caused friction with the FBI, which was concerned about ONI's poor evidence-handling procedures and violations of civil liberties. ONI's lack of arrest authority also hindered its efforts

---

[16] Packard, 17-19; Bath, 9-10; Dorwart, *Conflict of Duty*, 77.

[17] Columbia University, *The Reminiscences of Alan G. Kirk* (New York: Oral History Research Office, 1962), 183, Operational Archives, Naval Historical Center, Washington, DC. Cited hereafter as *Kirk Reminiscences*.

[18] Captain Ellis M. Zacharias, *Secret Missions; The Story of an Intelligence Officer* (New York, G. P. Putnam's Sons, 1946), 82. Zacharias retired from the naval service as a Rear Admiral.

[19] Dorwart, *Conflict of Duty*, 5.

in the security arena as they were required to coordinate with local or federal law enforcement to apprehend suspects.[20]

In 1937, Rear Admiral Ralston Holmes assumed duties as DNI and shifted the focus of effort at ONI to its positive intelligence mission. During his two years as DNI, he was responsible for obtaining a budget increase for ONI, expanding the attaché network, and improving the capabilities of the attachés by providing them with modern cipher equipment to encode their reports. His efforts were responsible for a doubling in attaché reporting during his tenure. He also increased liaison with the State Department and improved the Navy's operational security posture by winning support from then-CNO, Admiral William D. Leahy, to make ONI the final release authority for all information requests.[21] While still saddled with significant weaknesses, ONI was much better prepared for the coming war due to the changes implemented by RADM Holmes.

ONI Capabilities on the Eve of War

ONI principally focused its collection and analysis on the growing threat posed by Japan, also known as "Orange" in Navy war planning. Collection against this threat was difficult for a number of reasons. First, application of resources to this target was based simply on the "navy's deduction of what the country's [U.S.] interests were and its sea power doctrine," since there was no articulated strategy at the national level by which the navy could derive its strategic objectives.[22] Second, the Japanese were able to frustrate the efforts of ONI's most important collection source, its attaché force. Despite the increase in attachés that Holmes was able to obtain, the attaché office in Japan suffered from the Japanese policy of restricting access to its sensitive military facilities and the generally good operational security practiced by the Japanese. The Japanese also engaged in an active deception campaign, repeatedly denying they were building

---

[20] Dorwart, *Conflict of Duty,* 78-79. An interesting case study that illustrates this point is that of Harry Thomas Thompson, a former Navy Yeoman who was convicted of spying for the Japanese in July of 1936. FBI agents who assisted ONI with the investigation of Thompson wrote a scathing report to their superiors about the "strenuous" nature of Thompson's interrogation by ONI officers and the lack of quality in their investigative reports. For more information see: Special Agent R. P. Burruss, FBI Investigative report, January 7, 1936; Secretary of the Navy, Confidential Correspondence, RG 80; National Archives Building, Washington DC. (File, RG, and location cited hereafter as SECNAV-Confidential Correspondence); Special Agent John S. Bugas, FBI Investigative report (Information provided by LT A. H. McCollum and LT H. E. LeBarron), February 20, 1936, 1-2; SECNAV-Confidential Correspondence; Zacharias, 167; Dorwart, *Conflict of Duty,* 65-66.

[21] Bath, 19; Dorwart; *Conflict of Duty,* 94-98.

[22] George W. Baer, "U.S. Naval Strategy 1890-1945," *Naval War College Review* 44, no. 1, sequence 333 (Winter 1991): 18.

ships in violation of treaty limits, yet secretly building the *Yamato* class battleship and re-boilering older vessels behind large screens at their building docks.[23] Given this dearth of information, ONI analysts and collectors naturally applied their biases to assessments of Japanese capabilities, erroneously evaluating the quality of the Japanese naval fleet and their naval air forces as low.[24]

Despite the lack of success against the Japanese target, ONI's other HUMINT operations were more profitable. The American Legation, United States Naval Attaché, London (ALUSNA London), which will be discussed extensively in chapter 5, was a critical node for the flow of intelligence and technical information into ONI. ONI attachés in Latin America also had considerable successes in providing worthwhile intelligence and countering the moves of Axis intelligence operatives and subversive elements in the countries to which they were assigned.[25] By June of 1940, the Navy also took steps to strengthen its clandestine HUMINT capabilities and had relatively good success with these assets in North Africa and Mexico, although this capability would be absorbed by the Coordinator of Information (COI) the following year.[26]

SIGINT was also a major source of intelligence for ONI. The first Navy High Frequency Direction Finding (HF/DF) sites were established in 1918 and the U.S. had some success against foreign codes during the 1920s and 30s.[27] By the 1930s, the Navy and the Army had three major cryptologic collection sites located at Corregidor (Cavite or Station CAST) in the Philippines, Pearl Harbor, and Washington, DC.[28] The collection and decryption of the intercepted communications was handled by Director of Naval Communications OP-20-G, the "Communications Security Section," while much of the translation and analysis of the decrypted communications was handled by ONI.[29] While the Navy's cryptanalytic section was several times larger than the Army's at the start of the war, at around 147 personnel, the Navy had negligible success against the main Japanese naval code, designated JN-25, until just before the war, when cooperation with British communications intelligence (COMINT) personnel became more common.[30] Although information gathered from the Japanese diplomatic code was an important source of intelligence, it contained virtually no military infor-

---

[23] Malcolm Muir, Jr., "Rearming in a Vacuum: United States Navy Intelligence and the Japanese Capital Ship Threat, 1936-1945," *The Journal of Military History* 54, no. 4 (October 1990): 473-477.

[24] Muir, 478-479; Dorwart, *Conflict of Duty*, 27-29.

[25] Dorwart, *Conflict of Duty*, 106-109.

[26] Packard, 130.

[27] Aldrich, 33.

[28] Worth, 11-12.

[29] Jeffrey K. Bray, *Ultra in the Atlantic* (Laguna Hills, CA: Aegean Park Press, 1994), xii-xiv.

[30] Aldrich, 73.

mation and it was only distributed to a chosen few, which limited its utility as a source of information to inform operational planners and tactical forces.

Internecine Conflict and Its Effect on ONI

Patrick Beesly, who worked in the British Admiralty's Operational Intelligence Center (OIC) during World War II, has noted that one of the main deficiencies of ONI was its lack of any capability to provide operational intelligence (OPINTEL) support. He notes that the roots of this problem lay in World War I, when the Naval Intelligence Division (NID) of legendary British Rear Admiral Sir Reginald "Blinker" Hall, rather than ONI, provided the intelligence for the British and American operating forces. While the Royal Navy allowed its OPINTEL capability to lapse in the interwar period, it was able to reconstitute it quickly owing to the tradition initiated by Hall, whereas ONI had no such tradition to fall back on.[31] Another major difference between the NID and ONI, however, was that, on the eve of the war, ONI lacked direct access to key policymakers whereas the NID had direct access to the senior civilian and military leaders of the Royal Navy (the First Lord and the First Sea Lord of the Admiralty).[32] For the Americans, this situation also had its roots in the U.S. Navy's World War I experience and was largely a function of the personalities at the top of the Navy's hierarchy.

In August 1939, Admiral William Leahy was relieved by Admiral Harold "Betty" Stark as the Chief of Naval Operations (CNO). Stark was an officer in Admiral William Sims' planning cell during World War I and his ideas on how best to plan for naval operations were formed from that experience. ADM Sims had essentially created a miniature ONI to support planning done by his staff in London. For this reason, Stark accepted a model proposed by the Director of Naval War Plans, Rear Admiral Richmond Kelly Turner, which gave the War Plans Division the primary responsibility for evaluating intelligence.[33] Turner's reasoning was based on the fact that an intelligence assessment might cause an operational commander to take a specific course of action and, since potential ship movements fell under the purview of operators, they should have the final check on intelligence. Thus, in the period just prior to the war, the War Plans Division had primary responsibility for producing and disseminating intelligence

---

[31] Patrick Beesly, *Very Special Intelligence: The Story of the Admiralty's Operational Intelligence Center 1939-1945* (Garden City, NY: Doubleday & Company, INC., 1977), 111-112. Cited hereafter as Beesly, Very Special Intelligence.

[32] Bath, 4-5.

[33] Samuel E. Morison, *The Rising Sun in the Pacific, 1931-April 1942*, vol. 3 of *The History of United States Naval Operations in World War II* (Boston, MA: Little, Brown, and Company, 1948), 134-135, cited hereafter as Morison, *Rising Sun*; Jeffery M. Dorwart, *Office of Naval Intelligence: The Birth of America's First Intelligence Agency 1865-1918* (Annapolis, MD: Naval Institute Press, 1979), 124-125, cited hereafter as Dorwart, *ONI*; Dorwart, *Conflict of Duty*, 117; Packard, 16; Bath, 7.

assessments. By 1941, ONI was relegated to the position of reporting only factual information derived from their various collection sources. This situation was the source of acrimonious conflict between Turner and the DNI, RADM Kirk. Kirk fought vigorously for the reestablishment of ONI's preeminent position in the evaluation of intelligence, a position actually spelled out in regulation, but Stark preferred Turner's system.[34] The end result was that, by the time Kirk was relieved by Rear Admiral Theodore S. Wilkinson in October 1941, ONI was in a subordinate position to War Plans and was often out of the loop on the Navy's operations and war planning efforts prior to the war.[35]

Another source of internecine conflict that limited ONI's effectiveness was that which existed between ONI and OP-20-G. Once again, then-RADM Kirk was at the center of another controversy, this time with the Director of Naval Communications (DNC), who contended that the DNC, not ONI, should be the office to present decrypted "MAGIC" intercepts to the CNO and the Secretary of the Navy.[36] While Kirk won this battle and ONI was allowed to continue briefing the MAGIC decrypts, the conflict created considerable tension between ONI and OP-20-G that lasted through much of the pre-war period and beyond.

While ONI's capabilities were improving in the period just prior to the war, the British well understood they were attempting to engage in cooperative partner-ship with an organization they considered inferior. Beesly effectively sums up the major ONI deficiencies: "Where the Americans were far behind the British was in their general intelligence expertise, in inter-Service [and intra-Service] coopera-tion and co-ordination and effective use of results obtained from many different sources."[37] Despite its deficiencies, though, ONI became the main conduit for the sharing of intelligence with the British, through its attaché office in London, and was chosen as one of the main coordinators for technical exchanges between the two countries. While the British viewed their system of intelligence as superior to the Americans, they were also playing catch-up from the under-resourcing of the interwar period and had their own difficulties to overcome. An analysis of the state of British intelligence just prior to the war will demonstrate that it shared

---

[34] Arthur H. McCollum, *Reminiscences of Rear Admiral Arthur H. McCollum, U.S. Navy, Retired*, 1, United States Naval Academy Special Collections, 328-330, cited hereafter as *McCollum Reminiscences; Kirk Reminiscences*, 179-180, 182; Dorwart, *Conflict of Duty*, 155-161.

[35] Packard, 23; *McCollum Reminiscences*, 322-323.

[36] *Kirk Reminiscences*, 179; Packard, 22; John Winton, *Ultra in the Pacific: How Breaking the Japanese Codes and Cyphers Affected Naval Operations Against Japan, 1941-45* (Annapolis, MD: Naval Institute Press, 1993), 6-7. MAGIC was the code name used for decrypts of the Japanese PURPLE diplomatic code.

[37] Patrick Beesly, *Very Special Admiral: The Life of Admiral J. H. Godfrey, CB* (London: Ham-mish Hamilton, Ltd, 1980), 180. Cited hereafter as Beesly, *Very Special Admiral*.

many of the same problems of inter-Service rivalry and inadequate resources that beset U.S. intelligence.

Intelligence in The United Kingdom

British Intelligence Structure

Like U.S. intelligence in the 1930s, British intelligence consisted of a number of organizations. Also like the U.S., the British had a counterpart to ONI, the NID, and a Military Intelligence Division (MID), similar to the U.S. Army's organization of the same name. Additionally, since it had a separate Air Force, the British had an Air Intelligence Division to support that Service's requirements. Unlike the U.S., however, the British Foreign Office was much more active in intelligence matters than the U.S. State Department. In addition to its responsibility for overt diplomatic missions, the Foreign Office was also in charge of Britain's clandestine HUMINT activities and ran the Secret Intelligence Service (SIS), better known as MI6. Another feature that distinguished the British intelligence system from the American system was the use of inter-departmental intelligence branches to deal with intelligence functions that became more developed in the interwar period. Examples of these activities include: the Security Service (MI5), which handled domestic intelligence and counterintelligence; the Government Code and Cypher School (GC&CS), which dealt with all SIGINT matters; the SOE, with responsibility for covert action; the Political Warfare Executive, which analyzed foreign press and propaganda; and the Combined Services Detailed Interrogation Center, which dealt with Prisoner of War (POW) interrogations.[38]

British intelligence differed from the American system in one other important way, and that was in the area of interdepartmental coordination and cooperation. This is not to say there were no interdepartmental rivalries or friction among the component members, because, in this respect, the British system closely resembled the American one. Francis Hinsley, who wrote the official history of British intelligence during World War II, notes that prior to the war it was understandable how various intelligence departments, each of which had responsibilities to the central government and to their own organizations, "were naturally reluctant to exchange reliance on inter-departmental bodies for their own long-established control of the acquisition, the interpretation, and the use of whatever information

---

[38] Francis Hally Hinsley and others, *British Intelligence in the Second World War: Its Influence on Strategy and Operations 1* (London: Her Majesty's Stationery Office, 1979), 4, 90, cited hereafter as Hinsley, British Intel vol. 1; Alan Stripp, *Codebreaker in the Far East* (London: Frank Cass Publishers, 1989), 148; Smith, *Ultra-Magic Deals*, 20. The GC&CS was also known as Bletchley Park, the location where analysis of intercepted communications was conducted.

might bear on their work."[39] As with the American system, this led to duplication of effort and over-compartmentalization of intelligence, this despite the fact the British also had a titular head of intelligence, Sir Steward Menzies. Menzies or "C," who as head of the SIS and the GC&CS ran the two most substantial interdepartmental intelligence services for the British and held a position very much like that originally envisioned for the Director of Central Intelligence (DCI) in America. Like those of the DCI, his powers to bring about the cooperation or collaboration of the other branches of British intelligence were limited.[40]

While interdepartmental rivalries persisted throughout much of the interwar period, a growing realization that war was coming forced the various departments to reassess the need for better coordination among the intelligence services. To this end, the British formed a Joint Intelligence Sub-Committee (JIC) in June of 1936, the principal duty of which was to provide direct support to the Joint Planning Staff (JPS).[41] Although this was a major step in the coordination of intelligence, the JIC suffered from a number of problems. First, the Foreign Office refused to participate in the JIC, so a key component of British intelligence was not represented. Second, although the military services created the JIC to fill a need, they "effectively ensured that its work did not expand in such a way as to reduce the influence on policy and strategy which they individually derived from their responsibility for assessing intelligence for their own departments."[42] Finally, in a situation reminiscent of the conflict between the U.S. Navy's War Plans Division and ONI, the JPS did not use the JIC well as they "confined their enquiries to...routine or unanswerable requests...[since] on matters of first importance they regarded the co-ordination of intelligence and of intelligence with planning, as a process which they were capable of performing themselves."[43]

Although initially limited in its effectiveness, the JIC did develop into an important tool for the coordination and processing of intelligence by the time war came for England. The JIC was restructured in 1939, when the Foreign Office finally joined the organization and took on responsibilities for the JIC chairmanship. With that reorganization, the JIC took on many additional responsibilities, not the least of which were the responsibility for improving the efficiency of the

---

[39] Hinsley, *British Intel* vol. 1, 4.

[40] Menzies assumed duties as "C" following the death of Admiral "Q" Sinclair in November 1939. Sinclair had held that position throughout much of the 1920s and 30s. For additional information see Smith, *Ultra-Magic Deals*, 22-23; Ronald Lewin, *Ultra Goes to War* (New York: McGraw-Hill Book Company, 1978), 65-66.

[41] Hinsley, *British Intel* vol. 1, 36-38; Bath, 47.

[42] Hinsley, *British Intel* vol. 1, 38.

[43] Hinsley, *British Intel* vol. 1, 38.

British intelligence system and for drafting daily and weekly all-source intelligence summaries on the global situation for high-level decisionmakers.[44] Still, Hinsley contends that it took over a year after the war began before the various departments set aside their rivalries and began truly realizing the efficiencies the JIC was meant to reap.[45] As will be discussed in more detail in Chapter 7, the British would urge the U.S. to adopt a similar system in 1941, a development that became a minor irritant to leaders of U.S. intelligence.[46]

British Naval Intelligence

As expected, the primary British intelligence organization the U.S. Navy dealt with on a day-to-day basis was the Royal Navy's NID. The NID was founded in 1892 to provide intelligence that would support naval planning.[47] Like its U.S. counterpart, the organization shrank significantly in the post-World War I period and began the war sorely under-resourced. Divided into geographical bureaus that essentially did order-of-battle analysis, its principal sources of intelligence information were the British naval attachés, SIGINT, and a limited amount of photographic reconnaissance. To compound its problems, assignments with the NID, as with ONI, were not looked on as prestigious, so NID did not receive officers of the highest quality during the interwar period.[48] Two significant differences from ONI, however, were in the nature of the NID's relationship to its attachés and in its focus on Operational Intelligence. Unlike in ONI, the British naval attachés, even though they could communicate informally with the Admiralty and the NID, had to submit all official reports through the Foreign Office. The Foreign Office would pass the reports to the Admiralty but these reports would include the Foreign Office assessment, which sometimes differed significantly from that of the NID.[49]The formation of the NID's Operational Intelligence Center (OIC) was another major difference from ONI. Established in August 1939, this all-source fusion analysis center became a key component of the Allied victory in the battle of the Atlantic. Although the U.S. Navy developed a similar capa-

---

[44] Hinsley, *British Intel* vol. 1, 39-40, 42-43, 85.

[45] Hinsley, *British Intel* vol. 1, 3-4, 96, 292. Hinsley notes that although the war officially began with the invasion of Poland on 1 September 1939, it was not until February 1940 that all three Service Intelligence Directors attended a meeting of the JIC together. Hinsley blames the JIC's lack of effectiveness in the first year of the war to a limited vision of its potential and poor initiative on the part of the JIC leadership. See Hinsley, *British Intel* vol. 1, 93-96.

[46] Bath, 46.

[47] Beesly, *Very Special Intelligence*, 10; Hinsley, *British Intel* vol. 1, 6-7.

[48] Hinsley, *British Intel* vol. 1, 10, 103-107; Beesly, *Very Special Intelligence*, 7-10.

[49] Hinsley, *British Intel* vol. 1, 5-6, 11.

bility over time, its operational intelligence components were subordinate to the Fleet Commanders and the operations and planning sides of the Navy Staff.[50]

In addition to the NID and the JIC, there were three other British interdepartmental activities that would attempt to engage the U.S. Navy in closer intelligence ties during the interwar period. These were the GC&CS, the Far East Combined Bureau, and the SIS. Under the control of the Foreign Office and Sir Stewart Menzies, the day-to-day operations of the GC&CS were run by Commander Alistair Denniston. A truly interdepartmental effort, the British had consolidated all of their cryptographic resources into this organization following the Great War. In addition to analysis of "Y" signals (HF/DF and low-level ciphers), the GC&CS was responsible for breaking high-level military and diplomatic codes as well as designing the codes used by the British. In many respects, its responsibilities were similar to those of the present-day U.S. National Security Agency (NSA).[51] In addition to the interdepartmental organizations run in London, the British also established overseas intelligence centers in the Middle and Far East to foster coordination and cooperation between the intelligence organizations in those locales. The most significant of these to the U.S. Navy was the Far East Combined Bureau (FECB). Created in Hong Kong in 1935, the FECB moved to Singapore in 1939. While principally a SIGINT organization, predominantly manned by the Royal Navy, the FECB was technically responsible for coordinating all British Far East intelligence efforts and became the primary liaison to the cryptographers at U.S. Navy Station CAST in Corregidor, as cooperation between the two navies' intelligence organizations grew.[52] Finally, as will be detailed in chapter 6, the SIS was also interested in forging a closer relationship with ONI, principally in the area of counterintelligence. As documented in *British Security Coordination: The Secret History of British Intelligence in the Americas*, 1940-1945, the British SIS branch in New York City under Sir William Stephenson spearheaded an effort to actively engage U.S. intelligence agencies in closer cooperation with their British counterparts as part of

---

[50] For more information on the development, structure, and operation of the OIC see Patrick Beesly's excellent history of the OIC, *Very Special Intelligence*, xv, 1-2, 11-18, 19-23, 26-34, and 42-43; see also Hinsley, *British Intel* vol. 1, 12-13.

[51] For additional information on the development, structure, and operations of the GC&CS see: Stripp, 13-14, 150; Bath 10; Smith, *Ultra-Magic Deals*, 26-29; MacLachlan, 32.

[52] Aldrich, 20, 36; Bath, 139-140.

a larger effort to steer U.S. policymakers to enter the war on the side of Great Britain.[53]

---

[53] For additional information see British Security Coordination, *The Secret History of British Intelligence in the Americas, 1940-1945* (New York: Fromm International, 1999). Cited hereafter as BSC, *Secret History*. Richard Aldrich, in evaluating the cooperation between the intelligence services of both countries, has noted that the major deception orchestrated by the UK was convincing the U.S. that British intelligence was "second to none." See Aldrich, 100-101. The historical evidence shows Aldrich's assessment to be correct. While possessing a more sophisticated system, the British also had their own systemic problems and they contended with many of the same weaknesses they criticized in the U.S. system.

Chapter 2

U.S.-UK RELATIONS, 1914-1935:
FROM COOPERATION TO COMPETITION

The basis of friendship between the two great English-speaking peoples is rivalry and independence of each other, and these are the really true and lasting bases of all friendships. The instant the condition of dependence arises between two equals the essence of friendship is lost....There is no necessity for an alliance between Great Britain and the United States, and there probably never will be one, but, in effect, it exists, or must exist, through conditions which are arising in the world and which will hereafter necessitate that the two countries will stand together; otherwise they may fall together.

Captain Albert P. Niblack, USN, "Forms of government
in relation to their efficiency for war," *Proceedings*

The Historical Context

The quote above, written by the U.S. Director of Naval Intelligence following World War I, was both descriptive and prescient. While the alliance that would form between the U.S. and the UK between 1935 and 1945 would be one of the closest and most enduring the world has ever known, there were many in the U.S. who were far more focused on the rivalry that existed between the two states. Niblack's main argument concerned the commonalites and superiority of the U.S. and British forms of government and, while the development of the Fascist states of Europe and Asia was still years away, he correctly saw that it was the common values shared by the American and British people that would eventually overcome the tensions between the two countries.[54] What were the main sources of tension and why were they so significant in the inter-war period, particularly to the naval officer corps in both countries? First, even with the war experience behind them, many in the U.S. and the UK had little first-hand knowledge about each other and their perceptions of one another were rife with stereotypes and misconceptions. Second, while the seeds of naval operational and intelligence cooperation were planted during the period of the Great War, many U.S. naval officers saw the Royal Navy as their principal rival and the British felt threatened by a U.S. policy committed to building a "Navy second to none." Third, Great Britain was seen by many in the U.S. as representing colonialism, a practice most Americans despised, despite the fact that the U.S.

---

[54] Albert P. Niblack, CAPT, USN, "Forms of government in relation to their efficiency for war," *Proceedings* 46 (September 1920): 1402-1430.

had colonial possessions of its own. Fourth, the UK saw the U.S. as its main economic rival. This, coupled with a historic distrust of the ability of U.S. government officials to keep secrets, made the British hesitant to cooperate with the U.S. in the period after the Great War.

Stereotypes and Misperceptions

Stereotyping other peoples is always easy. For most Americans, the UK was seen as a class-based society, where birth mattered more than merit for one's advancement, and many held that the UK was not truly a democracy because their monarchial-parliamentary system did not resemble the republican form of government practiced in America. Additionally, America's revolutionary heritage, its large Irish immigrant population, and resentment of colonialism were all factors responsible for creating a feeling of distrust regarding British intentions and actions on the part of many Americans. This distrust was not a universal feeling, as many in the upper tier of American society idolized the British and there was significant respect for British cultural achievements at all levels of U.S. society.[55] Misperceptions also abounded in the UK and many in the ruling circles of that country were largely ignorant of how the U.S. functioned, both socially and politically, a condition that would persist throughout the interwar period and a factor that would later work against the British in their attempts to influence U.S. policy.[56]

Naval Rivalry and The Impact of Naval Arms Limitations

Naval Rivalry

U.S. participation in the Great War was a watershed event in U.S.-UK relations and, while the period under review in this chapter saw some easing of the tensions between the two countries, there were rough patches in the alliance which would serve as irritants in the future relations between the two navies. Despite the decision to enter the war on the U.S. side, Samuel Morison has noted that the leadership of the U.S. Navy was highly distrustful of the British. For example, before departing on his mission to England to coordinate the efforts of U.S. naval forces engaged in the war, Admiral William F. Sims was

---

[55] David Reynolds, *The Creation of the Anglo-American Alliance 1937-41: A Study in Competitive Co-operation* (Chapel Hill, NC: The University of North Carolina Press, 1982), 23-24; Smith, *Ultra-Magic Deals*, 1-2; Stephen Budiansky, "The Difficult Beginnings of U.S. British Codebreaking Cooperation," in *American-British-Canadian Intelligence Relations 1939-2000*, ed. David Stafford and Rhodri Jeffreys-Jones (Portland, OR: Frank Cass Publishers, 2000), 50-51.

[56] Reynolds, 12; Chief of Naval Operations (CNO), letter to Commander-in-Chief, U.S. Asiatic Fleet, 12 November 1940, Papers of Harold R. Stark, Operational Archives Branch, Naval Historical Center, Washington, D.C. Collection cited hereafter as *Stark Papers*.

told by the Chief of Naval Operations, Admiral William S. Benson, that he was not to "let the British pull the wool over your eyes" as America "would as soon fight the British as the Germans."[57] Despite this admonition, ADM Sims was able to overcome the tensions in the relationship with the British and the cooperation between the two naval services was much better than many expected it would be. The British were somewhat sensitive to U.S. concerns about being treated as the "junior partner" in the relationship but their ability to overcome these concerns was mixed at best. On the positive side, the British were very forthcoming with information that proved useful to the U.S., and later intelligence cooperation between the two navies took root here. The head of the NID during World War I, Rear Admiral "Blinker" Hall, while restricting access to his most important intelligence source — the decrypts that came from his SIGINT organization — was forthcoming in sharing intelligence with the U.S. on a range of topics from U-boat operations, to wireless communications, to counterintelligence information.[58] Despite this openness, many U.S. officers resented what they perceived, justifiably, as the British expectations that the U.S navy would conform to the British way of operating, an expectation that fed into the "institutional jealousy of the Royal Navy" that had existed within the U.S. naval officer corps since at least the war of 1812.[59]

This rivalry was not limited to the American side of the relationship and, in the period following the war, naval policy itself was a source of friction between the two countries. The two countries, and the other Great Powers of the world, were victims of applying concepts in both the Spanish-American War and the Russo-Japanese War that were first articulated by Alfred Thayer Mahan. The Mahanian principles, with their emphasis on the need to secure overseas bases and build large numbers of capital ships, had led to a costly naval arms race in the period prior to the Great War.[60] President Woodrow Wilson was a strong proponent of naval strength and he wished to resume a substantial naval building program after the war. This desire to build a "bigger Navy than hers [Great Britain] and do what we please," was seen as a form of blackmail by the British who could not afford to embark on another naval arms race and who felt their strategic requirements justified their possession of the world's largest and most powerful navy.[61] While the move to limit naval arms that started with the Harding administration in 1920

---

[57] Samuel E. Morison, *The Battle of the Atlantic, September 1939-May 1943*, vol. 1 of *The History of United States Naval Operations in World War II* (Boston, MA: Little, Brown, and Company, 1947), 38. Cited hereafter as Morison, *Battle of the Atlantic.*

[58] Dorwart, *ONI*, 101, 125-126; Bath, 6-9.

[59] Bath, 8-9; Michael Coles, "Ernest King and the British Pacific Fleet: The Conference at Quebec, 1944 ("Octagon"), *The Journal of Military History* 25, no. 1 (January 2001): 125.

[60] Baer, 8-10.

[61] Baer, 13-14; Morison, *Battle of the Atlantic*, xxxv; Reynolds, 15.

might be seen as a way to mitigate the tensions between the two navies, an analysis of the naval arms limitation effort shows that it actually created additional friction in the relationship.

The Impact of Naval Arms Limitation

For Warren Harding and subsequent administrations, the U.S. Navy was primarily seen as a diplomatic bargaining chip, as few outside the Navy saw any real potential for going to war with Great Britain or Japan, the two other strongest naval powers at the time.[62] While the move toward naval arms limitation appeared to be in consonance with the fiscal constraints the British were operating under in the post-war period, there was widespread distrust among the British as to American motives for holding the Washington Naval Conference of 1921-1922. James R. Leutze has correctly stated that it was "viewed by the Admiralty as an attempt by the Americans to win by treaty...what they had failed to win in the shipyards."[63] Just three months prior to the conference, the American ambassador to England reported that Winston Churchill had made an impassioned plea in Parliament to increase the British naval budget, noting it was the only way that the UK could "walk hand in hand with the United States not as a supplicant for protection but as an equal partner."[64] Clearly, the British saw the Washington Naval Conference not as a step toward general disarmament but as an attempt by the U.S. to curtail British power. For officers of the Royal Navy, who felt defense of the Empire required Britain to maintain the largest Navy in the world, the losses in tonnage and restrictions on capital ship construction agreed to at the conference would become a source of great frustration.

The end result of the Washington Naval Conference and the subsequent naval arms limitations conferences that would occur in the early 1930s became a major source of resentment for officers in the U.S. Navy as well. While the British did agree to parity with the U.S., the U.S. scrapped much more tonnage than the British and agreed to dismantle and stop construction on the newest U.S. capital ships. U.S. officers largely saw subsequent attempts by the British to exploit loopholes in the treaty concerning cruiser strength as an affront to the honest efforts the Americans had made to reverse the trend of rampant naval arms build-

---

[62] Baer, 15-17.

[63] James Richard Leutze, *Bargaining for Supremacy: Anglo-American Naval Collaboration, 1937-1941* (Chapel Hill, NC: The University of North Carolina Press, 1977), 4. Cited hereafter as Leutze, *Bargaining for Supremacy*.

[64] Department of State, "The Ambassador in Great Britain, letter to the Secretary of State, 4 August 1921," in *Foreign Relations of the United States, 1921 1* (Washington, DC: GPO, 1936): 51.

ups of the early 20th century.[65] The loss of American sea power prompted the future Secretary of the Navy, Frank Knox, to write a book entitled *The Eclipse of American Sea Power*, to address concerns on the part of the Navy that the "Admiralty...were laughing up their sleeve at having put it over us [and are] very anxious at the reaction....if American public opinion were adequately educated as to the results of the treaty."[66] While provisions were made to close some of the loopholes during the London Naval Conference in 1930, it was clear to naval officers on both sides of the Atlantic that the rivalry between them had only been exacerbated by their failed expectations regarding naval arms limitation.[67]

Although rivalry did not necessarily translate into fears that the two navies would one day clash, many American naval officers were wary of the British. Fleet Admiral Ernest King's attitudes were probably typical of the faction of U.S. officers who subscribed to the view that the British were not to be trusted. Even though some authors have noted that Naval War College war gaming against British forces was primarily designed to provide variety against the main ORANGE threat (Japan), and while others have cited naval officers at the time who contended that war with Great Britain was not a realistic possibility, the fact that King wrote his Naval War College thesis in 1932 on the premise that the U.S. Navy needed to be prepared to fight both the UK and Japan demonstrates that not all officers were quite so sanguine about the potential for peace between the two countries.[68] Although some have characterized King as a rampant Anglophobe, more balanced scholarship has demonstrated that it would be fair to say that he was pro-American rather than anti-British. His views were based on his appreciation of the American naval tradition and on his not being impressed with the performance of the Royal Navy in World War I, a navy which attempted to instruct the U.S. Navy in how to perform at sea, yet ran a porous blockade, fought an inconclusive engagement at Jutland, was slow to meet the submarine threat, and slow in adopting convoy operations.[69] Patrick Beesly, one of the foremost authors on British naval intelligence matters, in speaking of King, summarized the views of many in the U.S. Navy during the interwar period by stating that they were "devoted to [their] Service and determined that it should not again play second

---

[65] The ratio of naval arms reached at the conference was 5:5:3 (U.S.:UK:Japan). The U.S. scrapped 845,740 tons and some of her most modern warships, while the British scrapped a total of 605,975 tons. For additional information see: Morison, xxxvii, xlii; Coles, 125; Department of State, "The Treaty for the Limitation of Naval Armament," 21 November 1921, in *Foreign Relations of the United States 1922 1* (Washington, DC: GPO, 1936): 53-60, cited hereafter as FRUS 1922 vol. 1; "Statement Issued to the Press by the Conference on the Limitation of Armament," 15 December 1921, FRUS 1922 vol. 1, 130.

[66] Dorwart, *Conflict of Duty*, 24.

[67] Morison, xl; Coles, 126.

[68] Dorwart, *Conflict of Duty*, 139-140; Muir, 480; Coles, 126.

[69] Coles, 105-107, 125.

fiddle to the Royal Navy. If not actually anti-British...[they were] certainly not over-receptive to ideas and suggestions from the Admiralty."[70] Overcoming these attitudes on the part of senior naval leaders would prove a difficult task for the British as they sought to pursue closer cooperation with the U.S. prior to the formal entry of the U.S. into World War II.

Anti-colonialism and Wilsonian Idealism

Anti-Colonialism

Differing attitudes between the U.S. and the UK concerning colonialism were another major obstacle in the path of fuller cooperation between the two governments in the interwar period, and the tensions generated by these differing views persisted into the post-World War II timeframe. Many in America saw colonialism as one of the root causes of the Great War, which they saw as driven by competition between the Great Powers for overseas possessions. For most Americans, raised to idolize a cadre of enlightened leaders who had thrown off the shackles of British colonial rule in the 1700s, colonialism was an evil that curtailed the rights of people to live in free societies. While America did possess colonies, most Americans saw themselves as benevolent colonial rulers who were interested in promoting the trade and economic growth that would one day allow these colonies to transition to self-rule.[71] While this view may seem naive, given that the U.S. was involved in the economic exploitation of the areas under its control, people were inspired by the Wilsonian ideals of self-determination for all peoples and the U.S. was actively involved in a process of transitioning some of its significant colonial possessions, like the Philippines, to self-government in the 1930s. Economic rivalry was also a factor, as many believed British trade policies were part of a systematic attempt by the British to keep the U.S. out of foreign markets.[72] In addition to the influence of Wilsonian idealism, many in the U.S. naval officer corps opposed the British style of colonialism because they believed the British drive to retain its empire was poor strategy. Some

---

[70] Beesly, 112. Like Beesly, American naval officers looking retrospectively at the relationship between the two navies in the interwar period had greater sympathy for the position of their opposite numbers on the other side of the Atlantic than they probably possessed prior to the war. For example, VADM Kirk recalls how a couple of British cruisers approaching the Panama Canal in 1939 were forced to wait while a fleet of close to 100 U.S. warships transited through on their way to an exercise. Kirk realized "It was somewhat galling to their pride, that the Royal Navy, which always thought it could do whatever it liked anywhere, would have to be held up, and they were." See *Kirk Reminiscences*, 116-117.

[71] Coles, 113; John Charmley, *Churchill's Grand Alliance* (New York: Harcourt Brace & Company, 1995), 54.

[72] Charmley, 12-13.

firmly believed that British policies would create a pan-Asian, anti-white backlash in the Far East.[73] Historian John Charmley probably best summarized the American view of British colonialism when he stated that the "very speed with which the Japanese overran the British Empire in the Far East convinced many Americans that the British were not only imperialists, but bungling imperialists."[74]

Other Aspects of Wilsonian Idealism

Besides anti-colonialism, other principles of Wilsonian idealism were a source of friction for the British, as well. They were, in fact, economic rivals of the Americans, and they interpreted Wilsonian calls for increased free trade as extremely threatening and meant to consolidate and perpetuate the ascendancy of the U.S. in the post-World War I period.[75] British views on American anti-colonialism were colored by resentment because American ascendancy was also coupled with increasing American isolationism. Many resented a peace in Europe that they believed had been dictated to them by Wilson, yet when the time came to enforce an unworkable treaty, the Americans had chosen a path of disengagement.[76] In the minds of many British policymakers, Wilsonian idealism was a hollow concept and British Prime Minister Neville Chamberlain probably best summarized the prevailing view in England when he stated that "it is always best and safest to count on nothing from the Americans but words."[77]

Mesopotamia: Free Trade Advocacy and British Resentment

An excellent example of the tensions created by the two countries' differing views on Wilsonian principles can be found in the State Department's *Foreign Relations of the United States* series for 1920. Within three years of the war, the U.S. and the UK were engaged in a rather acrimonious dispute concerning the British mandate in Mesopotamia, modern-day Iraq, and the access to the oil concessions in that region. By the terms of the San Remo Agreement of 24 April 1920, the British and French had received various mandates in the Middle East under the provision that other countries would have fair and equal access to the

---

[73] Aldrich, 124.

[74] Charmley, 54.

[75] Charmley, 13. For a concrete example of the economic rivalry and how it extended to the actions of the U.S. Navy and ONI, Jeffrey Dorwart relates a story concerning Captain Frank Hill, U.S. Naval Attaché in Brazil during the 1920s. He states that "[a]pparently, much of their intelligence work went toward counteracting British influence, including outbidding Vickers and Armstrong to win a lucrative contract for Bethlehem Steel to repair Brazilian battleships." See Dorwart, *Conflict of Duty*, 137.

[76] Smith, *Ultra-Magic Deals*, 5-6.

[77] Charmley, 16.

resources of these areas.[78]At one point, the U.S. received word that there was a secret agreement between the British and French to exclusively exploit the resources of these mandates for their own purposes. In a letter to the British Ambassador, the U.S. Secretary of State, Bainbridge Colby, informed the UK that America expected the mandates to be "governed in such a way as to assure equal treatment in law and in fact to the commerce of all nations," and further stipulated that if a secret agreement existed between the British and the French it would "result in a grave infringement of the mandate principle, which was formulated for the purpose of removing...some of the principle [sic] causes of international differences."[79]

The British responded to the American concerns with a lengthy missive from the British Secretary of Foreign Affairs, Lord Curzon, which, although in diplomatic language, dismissed the concerns of the U.S. as irrelevant in this matter because the administration of Mesopotamia was a League of Nations matter and, since the U.S. was not a League member, it had no right to dictate policy to the British. The U.S. response was masterfully eloquent and diplomatic but it made clear to the British that the shortage of petroleum had created a situation whereby the U.S. would do what was needed to ensure free trade in the resources of Mesopotamia so that "the most enlightened principles recognized by states as appropriate for the peaceful ordering of their economic relations" could be followed.[80] In a response reminiscent of the recent diplomatic conflict between France and the U.S. over UN policy on Iraq, the U.S. essentially labeled as specious the British argument that their non-participation in the League of Nations curtailed their rights in this matter. The view in the U.S. was that

> [s]uch powers as the Allied and Associated nations may enjoy or wield, in the determination of the governmental status of the mandated areas, accrued to them as a direct result of the war against the Central Powers. The United States, as a participant in that conflict and *as a contributor to its successful issue*, cannot consider any of the associated powers...debarred from the discussion of its consequences.[81]

The U.S.'s selective withdrawal from international affairs amid increasingly isolationist sentiment culminated in the American Neutrality Laws, which

---

[78] Department of State, "The American Charge' to the Secretary General of the French Foreign Office—Aide Memoire," 7 August 1920, in *Foreign Relations of the United States, 1920* 2 (Washington, DC: GPO, 1936): 668. Cited hereafter as *FRUS 1920*, vol. 2.

[79] *FRUS 1920*, vol. 2, 658-659.

[80] *FRUS 1920*, vol. 2, 672.

[81] *FRUS 1920*, vol. 2, 671-672. Emphasis added by the present author.

became one of the primary sources of tension between the two countries even after the decision to engage in various cooperative endeavors had been reached.

British Security Concerns

The British also had concerns with U.S. security practices. The British felt that America's free and open society made it impossible for secret matters of state to remain secret for long. The power of the Congress and the Press were such that the British saw the U.S. government as an information sieve and concluded that anything shared with the U.S. would either find its way to the news media or to one of Britain's enemies. The British also saw U.S. intelligence capabilities as weak, particularly in the area of counterintelligence and counter-espionage.[82] Concerns in this area would act as a significant inhibitor on British decisions to engage in intelligence and technical exchanges with America and did inhibit greater cooperation in the period just before the start of World War II. The British decisions to use security concerns as an excuse to withhold information became a source of frustration and distrust on the part of senior U.S. naval and foreign-policy decisionmakers as the two countries moved closer in their relations before the war.

---

[82] Bath, 5; Dorwart, *ONI*, 24-26. The British were especially expert in U.S. counterespionage and operational security deficiencies as they routinely penetrated and bugged U.S. embassies, to include the embassy in London. See Martin S. Alexander, "Introduction," in *Knowing Your Friends: Intelligence Inside Alliances and Coalitions from 1914 to the Cold War*, ed. Martin S. Alexander (Portland, OR: Frank Cass Publishers, 1998), 3; Dorwart, *Conflict of Duty*, 24-26.

Chapter 3

U.S.-UK RELATIONS, 1935-1939:
THE BEGINNINGS OF A STRATEGIC RAPPROACHMENT

[O]bviously there is no political possibility here of "an agreement in con-tractual form" with Great Britain in the Orient. Whatever the euphemism this would in effect constitute an alliance.

> The Secretary of State to the Ambassador
> in Great Britain (Bingham), 29 June 1934,
> in *Foreign Relations of the United States 1934*

[British Prime Minister] MacDonald: We are interested in the political sit-uation in the Pacific which imposes certain risks on us that we did not have at the time of the London Treaty [of 1930] and we had hoped would not occur; we hoped that our cooperation with you would prevent it. But it did not work out that way.

> Minutes of Meeting Between British and American
> Delegations in the Prime Minister's Office at the
> House of Commons, 14 November 1934,
> in *Foreign Relations of the United States 1934*

Even as tensions continued between the U.S. and Great Britain during the interwar period, common interests also remained in place. As World War II drew closer, these interests would eventually overshadow the differences between the two countries and unite them in a common effort. Two areas of concern to the British and Americans were 1) countering the growing threat posed by Japan and 2) maintaining the naval ratios established in the Washing-ton Naval Treaty of 1921 and the London Naval Treaty of 1930. It is, therefore, not surprising that during the 1920s and early 1930s, exchanges of intelligence and technical information on these issues did occur. For the most part, however, these were conducted at a low level and concerned routine matters. The events surrounding the abortive London Naval Conference of 1935, which was not held due to a decision by Japan to abrogate its naval treaty commitments, dem-onstrated to the U.S. and Great Britain that their strategic concerns were grow-ing increasingly closer. As the situation in the Far East and Europe began to deteriorate, the British began to look to U.S. support as the most viable means of shoring up their strategic weaknesses.[83] By early 1938, secret talks between the world's two most powerful navies, conducted with the full approval of their respective governments, signaled the beginning of a series of intelligence cooperation and information exchange initiatives by the British to secure U.S. assistance in accomplishing their strategic objectives.

Precursor Intelligence Exchanges in The Interwar Period: 1920-1935

As he looked back on the early 1920s, Rear Admiral Royal Ingersoll, who played a pivotal role in the establishment of closer relations between the U.S. and British navies in 1938, remembered that relations with the British were generally cordial, although he could not recall specific details of any intelligence exchanges with the British during his time at ONI.[84] Another observer, Alan Harris Bath, a former Naval intelligence officer and the author of *Tracking the Axis Enemy*, finds that most of the cooperation during this period "consisted mainly of low-level operational exchanges carried out informally by American or British naval officers in the fleet or by naval attachés on foreign station."[85] Although there are indications of at least one formal meeting between representatives of the two navies in 1928 to discuss views on the Far East situation and the potential for cooperation, the present author's review of archival data supports Bath's assessment.[86] For example, information requests from the U.S. naval attaché in London to the NID show that the information exchanges between the two countries were very routine during this period. They included requests for information on such things as British naval pay scales, information on the pilots and equipment of the British "Fleet Air Arm," lists of ships removed from the Royal Navy active roster, lists of Royal Navy ships laid down and undergoing modernization, the practice and use of wireless telegraphy (W/T), information on W/T technology, coatings used for aircraft carrier decks, and deep-sea diving technology. In almost every case, these requests for information were framed as a "quid pro quo," with the U.S. naval attaché offering to provide similar information to the NID, if the NID honored the attaché's

---

[83] Lawrence Pratt, "Anglo-American Naval Conversations," *International Affairs* 47 (October 1972): 749, 754-758; Bath, 11-12; Coles, 114; Aldrich, 116, 122-124; Charmley, 58.

[84] *Ingersoll Reminiscences*, 47. RADM Ingersoll worked the ONI Japan desk from 1921 to 1924.

[85] Bath, 10.

[86] Dorwart, *Conflict of Duty*, 140; Bath, 10.

request.[87] This policy of quid pro quo was, and continues to be, standard practice for information exchanges between governments. As explained in Chapter 6, British decisions to forego quid pro quo in technical information and intelligence exchanges later became a major tool in their efforts to draw the U.S. into a closer relationship.

The Abortive London Naval Conference of 1935

The growing Japanese threat drove closer cooperation between the U.S. and the UK from 1931 to 1938. Japanese actions, such as the invasion of Manchuria in 1931, raised serious concerns in both countries, as many postulated that Japanese expansionism would eventually bring conflict between Japan and the Western powers in the Far East.[88] To further inflame the situation, the Japanese made it clear to the Americans and the British during the preliminary negotiations leading up to the London Naval Conference of 1935 that they intended to withdraw from their obligations under the various naval arms limitations treaties to which they were a signatory.[89] Japanese withdrawal from the treaties, which had kept the size of the Japanese Navy inferior to the navies of the U.S. and the UK, would permit the Japanese to build the fleet they needed to challenge U.S. and British naval dominance in the Pacific. Jeffery Dorwart writes that the events surrounding the London Naval Conference of 1935 were a watershed moment in the history of the relationship between the U.S. and Great Britain, marking the beginning of the rapprochement between the two countries.[90] The present author's independent analysis of these events using the diplomatic correspondence from that period, as related below, demonstrates that Dorwart's contention is correct.

The U.S. sent its delegation for the London Naval Conference to the UK some six months prior to the beginning of the conference in an attempt to lay a com-

---

[87] CAPT W. W. Galbraith, USN, Naval Attaché, Letter to Sir Oswyn A. R. Murray K.C.B., The Admiralty, 6 January 1930; Division of Naval Intelligence General Correspondence, 1929-1942, RG 38, National Archives Building, Washington, DC, cited hereafter as *DNI Correspondence*; CAPT W. W. Galbraith, USN, Naval Attaché, Letter to Sir Oswyn A. R. Murray K.C.B., The Admiralty, 2 July 1930, *DNI Correspondence*; CAPT W. W. Galbraith, USN, Naval Attaché, Letter to Squadron Leader A. R. Boyle, Air Ministry, 2 July 1930, *DNI Correspondence*; CAPT W. W. Galbraith, USN, Naval Attaché, Letter to Sir Oswyn A. R. Murray K.C.B., The Admiralty, 2 July 1930, *DNI Correspondence*; CAPT W. W. Galbraith, USN, Naval Attaché, Letter to Sir Oswyn A. R. Murray K.C.B., The Admiralty, 21 July 1931, *DNI Correspondence*; CAPT W. S. Anderson, USN, Naval Attaché, Letter to Sir Oswyn A. R. Murray, G.C.B., The Admiralty, 21 June 1934, DNI Correspondence; CAPT Herbert S. Howard, USN, Acting Naval Attaché, Letter to Sir Oswyn A. R. Murray, G.C.B., The Admiralty, 7 August 1935, DNI Correspondence.

[88] Morrison, *Battle of the Atlantic*, xl.

[89] *Ingersoll Reminiscences*, 68.

[90] Dorwart, *Conflict of Duty*, 138.

mon framework for negotiation with the British, which would give both countries a better bargaining position against the Japanese. At the start of negotiations, U.S. and British goals for the conference were diametrically opposed. Norman Davis, the Chairman of the U.S. Delegation, was given orders by Franklin Roosevelt to pursue a 20 percent across-the-board reduction for naval forces and a 10- to 15-year extension to the terms of all existing naval arms limitations treaties then in effect. If the 20 percent reduction could not be attained, the fallback position was to have the British agree to maintain parity with the U.S. in naval forces.[91] President Roosevelt instructed Davis to present the U.S. goals personally to Prime Minister MacDonald, and to argue that the reduction in forces was needed to ease tensions in the world. Other factors, such as fiscal constraints and American isolationist sentiments, were most likely just as significant in Roosevelt's decision to advocate for naval force reductions.[92] Reporting on his conversations with MacDonald to the President and Secretary of State, Cordell Hull, Davis reported that the British had actually been hoping the U.S. would agree to an increase in British naval forces and they believed the U.S. did not truly understand how much the world situation had changed since the last naval arms limitations talks, which had been held in London in 1930. In particular, the British desired a substantial increase in their cruiser strength, telling Davis that "in 1930 England and America faced a single problem, namely, the Japanese; whereas today America still faces only this single problem, England now also faces the acute problem of Europe which is relatively academic to the United States."[93] Although both sides seemed diametrically opposed, within a few months of these conversations the differences in U.S. and the UK positions would become irrelevant in the face of the need to develop a common understanding of how best to respond to Japan's decision to abrogate its treaty obligations.

The development of this common understanding would take place in the context of a series of frank discussions between the American and British delegations, some of which were attended by the British Prime Minister. As winter approached, negotiations no longer focused on U.S. desires to reduce naval forces because the Japanese decision had made that position untenable for the Americans. During a discussion in November 1934, the British did attempt to get the U.S. to agree on a position concerning higher "qualitative" limits on naval cruiser strength, but the U.S. delegation remained noncommittal. The major concern of

---

[91] The Ambassador in Great Britain (Bingham) to the Secretary of State, 19 June 1934, in *Foreign Relations of the United States 1934 1* (Washington, DC: GPO, 1951), 262. Cited hereafter as *FRUS 1934* vol. 1. This cable, released by Ambassador Bingham, was actually from Norman Davis.

[92] The Secretary of State to the Ambassador in Great Britain (Bingham), 26 June 1934, in *FRUS 1934* vol. 1, 277.

[93] The Ambassador in Great Britain (Bingham) to the Secretary of State, 27 June 1934, in *FRUS 1934* vol. 1, 279.

the Americans was the issue of parity with the British now that the Japanese were about to embark on a new naval building program. Prime Minister MacDonald emphatically assured the American delegation that parity with the U.S. Navy would remain the policy of the UK, despite Japanese actions, but progress on a common approach to meet the destabilizing situation in the Orient was desperately needed.[94] The U.S. agreed that some system for collective security in the Pacific was required. The British concurred with this assessment but made it clear their view was that collective security could only be maintained through a credible deterrent and it was the responsibility of the U.S. and the UK "to terrorize the rest of the world into giving great moral answers to great moral issues."[95] While noting that he understood this position, Davis told the British that embarking on a large-scale naval building program would be difficult for the U.S. as neither the American people nor the Congress were in favor of expanding the Navy.[96] Even though both sides left the meeting agreeing to the need for a common understanding, it was obvious that the internal political situation in America would continue to be a major factor in curtailing U.S. freedom of action in foreign policy, a factor which would continue to adversely affect the relationship between the two countries until the Pearl Harbor attack.

Davis reported the substance of these conversations to his superiors in Washington. It is evident from the responses sent to him by Cordell Hull that the Japanese actions had persuaded U.S. decisionmakers to pursue closer cooperation with the British on the Far East situation. This does not mean that distrust of the British had evaporated. When presented with news that the British had offered to be intermediaries with the Japanese in trying to resolve the dilemma the prospect of Japanese rearmament had created, Hull warned Davis that this would be unacceptable. Were the British to pursue that policy, U.S. public opinion would rapidly turn against them as Americans would interpret the British-Japanese negotiations as an attempt on the part of the British to reinvigorate their previous alliance with the Japanese.[97] Still, Hull's thinking on the matter of cooperation with the British evolved considerably from that expressed in the epigraph which began this chapter. While warning Davis that the current talks with the British were not to be a negotiation, it was clear to him now that the U.S. must "expend our best efforts to bring about an early, open and conclusive indication of align-

---

[94] Minutes of Meeting Between British and American Delegations in the Prime Minister's Office at the House of Commons, 14 November 1934, in *FRUS 1934* vol. 1, 334-337. Cited hereafter as Meeting Minutes, 14 November 1934, *FRUS 1934* vol. 1.

[95] Meeting Minutes, 14 November 1934, *FRUS 1934* vol. 1, 338.

[96] Meeting Minutes, 14 November 1934, *FRUS 1934* vol. 1, 339.

[97] The Secretary of State to the Chairman of the Delegation (Davis), 17 November 1934, in *FRUS 1934* vol. 1, 354. Cited hereafter as Secretary of State, 17 November 1934, *FRUS 1934* vol. 1.

ment between the British and ourselves" on the Japanese problem.[98] Days later Hull would tell Davis that "[c]ooperation with the British is something we earnestly desire" but successful cooperation would depend on the British ability to engage in "'give' and 'take'" on matters of policy.[99] While there were no substantive steps toward alliance following the failure of the 1935 London Naval Conference, Dorwart is correct in asserting this was a key moment in the relations between the U.S. and the UK and marked a major step on the road to fuller cooperation on mutual strategic concerns.

The Ingersoll Mission of 1938

By 1937, the situation in Europe and the Far East had continued to deteriorate and, in response, America had become increasingly isolationist. Public opinion clearly showed that most Americans wanted to avoid the coming conflict and, to this end, Congress passed strict neutrality laws in 1935, 1936, and 1937. While isolationists were in the majority, some like Admiral Harry E. Yarnell, Commander of the U.S. Asiatic Fleet, saw war between totalitarianism and democracy as inevitable and he believed decisive action was needed if the democracies were to survive the coming struggle intact.[100] For Great Britain, with her proximity to Europe and her vast colonial possessions, the events of 1937 would create a strategic dilemma of significant proportions. In the summer of that year the Japanese began their assault on China, Mussolini rejected British attempts to reach an accommodation with Italy over Ethiopia, and it was evident the Germans were rapidly rearming. Faced with threats in numerous areas of national interest, the British were still two years away from completing their rearmament goals.[101]

The dilemma the British faced in the autumn of 1937 was tied to the naval policies of the 1920s and 30s, which had restricted the growth of the Royal Navy. While Great Britain had enough assets to send a sizeable force to the Far East to counter the Japanese, planners on the naval staff questioned if the force was large enough as it would, at best, give them parity with the Japanese fleet. Even if this fleet were large enough to deter Japanese adventurism, deploying it to the Far East would leave England exceedingly vulnerable in the Mediterranean and the Atlantic at a time when tensions in Europe were increasing. The British could have sent a smaller force to their stronghold at Singapore, but many felt this would be seen as a provocation by the Japanese, and the relative weakness of such a force might incite the Japanese to attack. By November of 1937, the Brit-

---

[98] Secretary of State, 17 November 1934, *FRUS 1934* vol. 1, 354.

[99] The Secretary of State to the Chairman of the American Delegation (Davis), 8 Dec 1934, *FRUS 1934* vol. 1, 391.

[100] Dorwart, *Conflict of Duty*, 86.

[101] Pratt, 746.

ish Foreign Secretary, Anthony Eden, became convinced that the only way to resolve this dilemma would be to secure an agreement with the U.S. on cooperation in the event of war with Japan.[102] Not everyone agreed with Eden. In October of 1937, Roosevelt had made a speech in which he discussed the concept of a "quarantine" to be enforced against aggressive states, such as Japan. The British felt this to be an ill-defined policy and Admiral Chatfield, the First Sea Lord, felt that cooperation with the U.S. would be fruitless as he believed the U.S. would "stand aside" if the British came into conflict with the Japanese in the Far East.[103]

Despite the opposition, on 27 November 1937 Eden directed the British Ambassador in the U.S., Sir Ronald Lindsay, to engage the Americans on the issue of cooperation in the Far East. Lindsay's initial approach, to Secretary of State Cordell Hull, and Undersecretary of State Sumner Welles, was rejected despite a desire on the part of the then CNO, ADM Leahy, and ADM Yarnell to discuss the matter with the British.[104] The situation changed on 12 December 1937, when the Japanese attacked the *Panay*, an American gunboat that was operating in Chinese waters. Following the *Panay* incident, the British Foreign Office pressed Lindsay to reengage the Americans and he was given an audience with Roosevelt and Hull in which he once again made a pitch for increased cooperation between the two countries on the Japanese threat. Despite objections from Hull, Roosevelt approved secret staff talks between the navies of both countries.[105] To maintain the secrecy of this mission, one man, the Navy's Director of War Plans, Captain Royal Ingersoll, was chosen as the U.S. negotiator for meetings that were to take place in London as soon as CAPT Ingersoll could arrive there. Ingersoll recalls that he was given specific orders by the President to "make preliminary arrangements, if we could, with the British for joint action in case of war with Japan."[106] While the press and Congress expressed interest in Ingersoll's departure and return to the U.S., ADM Leahy maintained the secrecy of the staff talks by claiming they concerned the routine matter of obtaining "information from the British Admiralty on the methods used for computing exact tonnages of Men of War."[107] While members of Congress were very concerned about the Ingersoll Mission, Congressman Carl Vinson, Chairman of the Naval Affairs Committee, ran interference for ADM Leahy and assured him he would not be required to answer any Congressional inquiries on the matter. This greatly

---

[102] Pratt, 746-748.

[103] Pratt, 747.

[104] Bath, 14; Pratt, 749.

[105] Leutze, *Bargaining for Supremacy*, 18-20; Bath 14-15; Pratt, 750-752.

[106] *Ingersoll Reminiscences*, 70.

[107] Stephen T. Early, Secretary to the President, to Roosevelt, 28 January 1938, in *Franklin D. Roosevelt and Foreign Affairs, December 1937-February 1938 4*, ed. Donald B. Schewe (New York: Garland Publishing, Inc., 1979), 795.

assuaged British concerns about the publicity surrounding Ingersoll's mission, since they feared an anti-British backlash in America if the true nature of Ingersoll's visit were discovered.[108]

Ingersoll arrived in London on 31 December 1937 and linked up with the U.S. Naval Attaché, Captain Russell Willson, who would accompany him during the staff talks with the British. On 1 January 1938, Ingersoll met with Eden and with the Deputy Chief of the Admiralty Naval Staff, VADM James. Ingersoll made it clear to all concerned that he was unable to negotiate a formal agreement between the two governments and his mission was "to obtain naval information on which to plan and to base decisions, if necessary, for future action."[109] On 3 January, Ingersoll met with ADM Chatfield and his opposite number on the Admiralty staff, CAPT Phillips. After some general discussions on the strategic nature of the situation in the Far East, the British very frankly laid out the strategic situation for Ingersoll, providing him with detailed information on the size and composition of the force they could send to the Far East, the disposition of the forces they had there, and the status of Singapore. Realizing how important the exchange of information would be for any coordinated actions, Chatfield told Ingersoll that it was "desirable to arrange early the means of communication and the exchange of intelligence between the two fleets."[110] To this end, Ingersoll discussed with Phillips the need for a set of codes that could be used to conduct these information exchanges. Furthermore, he recommended expanding intelligence exchanges with the British, stating that

> exchange of information by informal agreement is now taking place
> between the British Director of Naval Intelligence and Willson regarding
> Japanese naval construction and the Mandated Islands. The British
> believe this should be extended now to include movements and location
> of Japan's naval units.[111]

While this type of operational intelligence exchange may have already been occurring on a limited basis between the U.S. Asiatic Fleet and the British China Fleet, the offer to begin formalizing some of these intelligence

---

[108] Royal Ingersoll, CAPT, USN, Letter to Captain Russell Willson, USN, 21 February 1938, in the U.S. Naval Academy Library microfilm collection, *Strategic Planning in the U.S. Navy: Its Evolution and Execution 1891-1945* (Wilmington, DE: Scholarly Resources, Inc., 1979). Collection cited hereafter as *Strategic Planning*.

[109] Royal Ingersoll, CAPT, USN, Memorandum for the Chief of Naval Operations, 31 December 1937, *Strategic Planning*, 1-2.

[110] Royal Ingersoll, CAPT, USN, Memorandum for the Chief of Naval Operations, 3 January 1938, *Strategic Planning*, 1-2.

[111] Royal Ingersoll, CAPT, USN, Memorandum for the Chief of Naval Operations, 3 January 1938, *Strategic Planning*, 1-4.

exchanges was a key step in the process of expanding intelligence cooperation between the two countries.[112]

The remainder of Ingersoll's mission was spent working out the details of how cooperation between the two navies would work in the event of war with Japan. The British offered to provide the codes and ciphers needed to facilitate secure communications between the two fleets and the U.S. was given detailed information on the British radio network and the specific frequencies used by the British forces. Plans for a distant blockade, designed to contain the Japanese, were discussed and finalized. The British would take the western Pacific from Singapore to New Zealand and the U.S. would be responsible for the eastern Pacific. Although the Record of Conversation detailing the discussions contains a number of qualifiers with regard to when this plan would be implemented, it was still a significant achievement given the level of distrust that still pervaded U.S.-UK relations.[113]

While the Ingersoll Mission set the stage for improved cooperation between the U.S. and the UK, what were its immediate results? Ingersoll believed the mission, while limited in its immediate impact, did create the conditions for the successful coordination of British and U.S. naval action by establishing combined codes and, eventually, liaison officers in the various fleets.[114] Ingersoll also advocated continuing the process of engagement and recommended a regular schedule for staff talks between the U.S. and the UK. His suggestion was rejected by the U.S. Navy's leadership, however, because the Navy feared Congress would focus its attention on them if staff talks were to become a regular occurrence. Given the intense isolationist sentiment in the U.S., the Navy was not willing to risk the public backlash that might result from revelations concerning the secret talks with the British.[115] So, while the Ingersoll Mission may have had some positive long-term effects, its immediate results with regard to improving cooperation between the British and the U.S. were not so impressive.

---

[112] For information on how the ADM Yarnell and the Asiatic Fleet may have cooperated with the British during this period see Pratt, 750.

[113] Royal Ingersoll, CAPT, USN, Memorandum for the Chief of Naval Operations, 5 January 1938, *Strategic Planning*, 1-4; Royal Ingersoll, CAPT, USN, Memorandum for the Chief of Naval Operations, 10 January 1938, *Strategic Planning*, 1-4; Royal Ingersoll, CAPT, USN, Memorandum for the Chief of Naval Operations, 12 January 1938, *Strategic Planning*. Russell Willson, CAPT, USN, Memorandum for the Director of Naval Intelligence, 10 February 1938, *Strategic Planning*.

[114] *Ingersoll Reminiscences*, 72-76.

[115] Russell Willson, CAPT, USN, Letter to Captain Royal Ingersoll, 4 March 1938, *Strategic Planning*, n.p; Royal Ingersoll, CAPT, USN, Letter to Captain Russell Willson, 29 March 1938, *Strategic Planning*. Reynolds, 60.

In the area of intelligence exchange, the Ingersoll Mission also seemed to promise a new chapter in the relationship between the two navies. Unfortunately, distrust continued to be a common feature of the relationship and intelligence and technical information exchange would not improve significantly in the period immediately following the Ingersoll Mission. In February 1938, the U.S. Naval Attaché, CAPT Willson, was instructed to pursue a more aggressive information exchange policy with the British. Willson was successful in securing some general information on British fleet tactics, but his requests for information on the defenses of Singapore and on harbor boom defenses were denied by the British because the U.S. would not release information on its Norden bombsight or on the arresting-gear capabilities of its aircraft carriers.[116] Attempts by the British Air Attaché in Washington, DC to obtain information on the Norden bombsight, perhaps the most closely held piece of technology the U.S. possessed in the interwar period, were also rebuffed by ONI.[117] Although both countries encouraged a more liberal intelligence-exchange policy following the Ingersoll Mission, quid pro quo was still the criteria for these exchanges, which seriously impeded the flow of information. While the policy divisions (plans and intelligence) wanted a greater level of exchange, they were often overruled by the technical divisions, such as ordnance, which were fearful of hard-earned technical secrets getting into the wrong hands.[118] Despite the restrictions, exchanges on seemingly mundane matters like personnel issues gave the U.S. some insight into British capabilities. For example, even though the NID was not allowed to share any information about anti-submarine technical equipment with the U.S. naval attaché, Willson surmised the British must have been successful in developing these capabilities during the interwar period as he had received detailed knowledge about the substantial number of "Submarine Detectors" (Sonarmen) in the British fleet.[119] With restrictions like these in place, however, substantive progress on the exchange of intelligence would require a major policy shift on the part of at least one of the participants to release both sides from the tyranny of the quid pro quo paradigm. That shift did not occur until after the beginning of the war.

---

[116] James R. Leutze, "Technology and Bargaining in Anglo-American Naval Relations: 1938-1946," *Proceedings* 103, no., sequence 892 (June 1977): 51-52, cited hereafter as Leutze, "Technology and Bargaining"; Leutze, *Bargaining for Supremacy*, 31-33; David Zimmerman, *Top Secret Exchange: The Tizard Mission and the Scientific War* (Montreal: McGill-Queen's University Press, 1996), 27-28.

[117] G.C. Pirie, Group Captain, Air Attaché, Letter to Director of Naval Intelligence, 28 May 1938, *DNI Correspondence*. Commander F. T. Spellman, Bureau of Ordinance, Memorandum to the Director of Naval Intelligence, 21 June 1938, *DNI Correspondence*.

[118] Leutze, *Bargaining for Supremacy*, 31.

[119] Russell Willson, CAPT, USN, Letter to Captain Alan G. Kirk, 23 September 1938, *Papers of Alan G. Kirk*, Operational Archives Branch, Naval Historical Center, Washington, D.C.

Cautious Approaches to Cooperation in 1939

The Ingersoll Mission opened the door to greater cooperation between the U.S. and British navies, but the U.S. was placated by the apologetic Japanese response to the *Panay* incident. Moreover, the fervor that had driven the movement to explore closer cooperation with the British had waned over the course of 1938. Still, by January of 1939, the worsening situation in Europe forced the British to realize that sending a naval force sufficient to deter the Japanese and protect its Far East possessions was now beyond its capabilities, given the priority of the Mediterranean and the Atlantic theaters. This was revealed to the Americans through their naval attaché, CAPT Willson, when he asked the Admiralty if they desired to update the Record of Conversation they had developed with Ingersoll.[120]

Although the British had hoped to send a smaller force to the Far East in the event of war, their planners came to the conclusion by the spring of 1939 that even the dispatch of a modest force would be a strategic impossibility given the threatening situation in Europe. Given this substantial change in their war planning, the Admiralty dispatched Commander T. C. Hampton, from the Admiralty War Plans Division, to Washington to update the Americans on their situation. During two secret visits to the personal home of the CNO on 12 and 14 June 1939, Hampton described the changes the British were required to make to the Record of Conversation established by the Ingersoll Mission, and attempted to ascertain the limits of U.S. cooperation given the new strategic environment.[121]

Beesly has contended there were no substantive results from these talks.[122] Although that may be true from one perspective, the records of the conversations drafted by the War Plans Division Directory, Rear Admiral Robert L. Ghormley, are informative in that they reveal how crucial the cooperation of the U.S. had become to British war planners. It is evident that the British now saw U.S. support as their best alternative for mitigating their strategic weakness. Once again, the British revealed these weaknesses to Leahy and Ghormley with exceptional candor, relaying the fact the British could not send a fleet to the Far East in event of war with Japan. Great Britain's response in that eventuality would be to secure the Mediterranean first, which would allow it the freedom of action needed to reinforce the Far East. Hampton then attempted to ascertain the limits of U.S. cooperation and, in the process, discussed concessions the British would be willing to make in exchange for U.S. assistance. For example, he made

---

[120] Russell Willson, CAPT, USN, Record of Conversations in London 13 January 1939 in Connection with Bringing Up-to-date the Ingersoll Conversations in London, January 1938, 17 January 1939, *Strategic Planning*, 1-4.

[121] Reynolds, 60-62; Bath, 23.

[122] Beesly, *Very Special Admiral*, 172.

clear to the Americans that if they were involved with the British in a war against Japan, all British Far East ports would be open to them and that leadership of any joint action "would doubtless...be vested in the Commander of the larger force," thus making it clear that the British understood U.S. sensitivities about their "junior partner" status in the Great War.[123] Significantly, from an intelligence perspective, Hampton also revealed details concerning the British HF/DF network in the Far East and, even more significantly, described the major weakness of the system as the fact the network lacked "good angles" for cross-fixing contacts, but that the British felt adding the capabilities of their network to those of the U.S. would be of advantage to both countries.[124] As with the offer to exchange intelligence on Japanese naval movements during the Ingersoll visit, this was another attempt on the part of the British to use the prospect of closer intelligence cooperation as one component of a many-layered approach designed to entice the U.S. into a closer partnership.

Since these were not official talks, Leahy remained noncommittal, only revealing his personal view that the U.S. would remain neutral as long as possible but assuring Hampton that, in the event of war, the U.S. would position its fleet in Hawaii to deter Japanese aggression against U.S. interests, and that the U.S. would conduct air and sea patrols of the Western Atlantic, particularly in the Caribbean and the Panama Canal Zone, to protect U.S. interests.[125] On 14 June, Hampton again met with Leahy and Ghormley to clarify some of the points raised during the 12 June meeting. Principally, he desired to understand more about the U.S. role in the Pacific and the Atlantic, inquiring whether the U.S. would be willing to take the lead in the Pacific theater in the event of combined action against the Axis. Once again, Leahy offered his personal opinion, stating that the U.S. would take the lead in the Pacific and that he expected the British to take the lead in the Atlantic theater except in the case of local submarine patrol areas off the U.S. coast and in the Caribbean and the Panama Canal Zone.[126] While it is correct to say these talks produced no tangible results, they were important for another reason. First, they indicate that the concerns that drove both countries to engage in the Ingersoll Mission were still valid over a year later. Second, they clearly show that the British had come to the inescapable conclusion that the best, and possibly only, solution for their strategic dilemma was a cooperative, intelligence-intensive partnership with America.

---

[123] Robert L. Ghormley, RADM, USN, Memorandum of an Informal Conversation Held at the Residence of the Chief of Naval Operations at 1700, 12 June 1939, *Strategic Planning,* 3. Cited hereafter Ghormley Memorandum, 12 June 1939.

[124] Ghormley Memorandum, 12 June 1939, *Strategic Planning,* 3.

[125] Ghormley Memorandum, 12 June 1939, *Strategic Planning,* 1-2.

[126] Robert L. Ghormley, RADM, USN, Memorandum of an Informal Conversation Held at the Residence of the Chief of Naval Operations at 1700, 14 June 1939, *Strategic Planning,* 1-2.

Chapter 4

KEY U.S. POLICYMAKERS AND THEIR
ATTITUDES TOWARD COOPERATION

The three main policymakers with regard to naval matters were the President, Franklin Roosevelt; Secretary of the Navy Frank Knox; and the Chief of Naval Operations, ADM Stark. Some authors have accused these three men of being anglophiles or pawns of the British, but these arguments have little validity. In reality, all three were realists who saw that aiding England was in the national interests of the U.S. and was the path most in consonance with U.S. values. Despite their inclination to assist the British, even as they were in pursuit of U.S. foreign policy objectives, all three men were constrained by the domestic political situation and their own mistrust of British intentions in forging a closer partnership.

Franklin Delano Roosevelt

Although some have assumed Roosevelt was an anglophile because of his familial connections to England and his patrician upbringing, the reality is more complex. True, Roosevelt did have cultural affinity with the British, but his attitude toward British policies was circumspect. Partly this was rooted in his deep-seated anti-colonialism. Like many Americans, he saw colonialism as a major causal factor behind World War I and he believed that the desire of the British and other European countries to maintain colonial possessions would lead to more wars in the future. Furthermore, Roosevelt had a strong, general distrust of the British and greatly resented the way they treated America as a junior partner.[127] A telling example of this can be found in "off the record" remarks he made to a group of reporters upon hearing that British newspapers were calling his idea of a "quarantine" to contain Japanese aggression in 1937 "an attitude without a program."[128] In response, Roosevelt revealed his exasperation with the British by asserting that if the British had a better idea, they needed to state it, and by complaining that "[e]verytime we enter into some kind of effort to settle something with our British friends, when we make the suggestion[,] they get 90% and we get 10%."[129] Clearly, Roosevelt's attitudes toward colonialism and his unhappiness with the lack of perceived U.S. equality by the British were two factors that

---

[127] Reynolds, 25; Aldrich, 122-123.

[128] "Press Conference, Hyde Park, 6 October 1937," in *Franklin D. Roosevelt and Foreign Affairs, January 1939-August 1939*, Donald B. Schewe, ed. (New York: Garland Publishing, Inc., 1979).

[129] "Press Conference, 6 October 1937" in *Franklin D. Roosevelt and Foreign Affairs, January 1939-August 1939.*

in his mind worked against closer cooperation, unless that cooperation could be enacted on terms favorable to the U.S. and consistent with American values.

Even if Roosevelt had been in favor of unrestricted assistance to the British prior to the war, the domestic political situation would not allow it. The American public was largely isolationist in its outlook and this had a tremendous impact on the President's foreign policy. Even Roosevelt's articulation of the quarantine concept in 1937, with its emphasis on cooperative, defensive action to contain aggression, was in strong contradiction to pacifist groups interested in preserving U.S. neutrality.[130] Even after war had come in September of 1939, Roosevelt's freedom of action was restricted by re-election pressures and the requirement to observe U.S. neutrality laws, which in particular put significant restrictions on arms sales and the movement of U.S. military and commercial assets into designated war zones.[131]

Still, Roosevelt and his advisors saw aid to England as being in the best interests of the U.S., and they were willing to push and bend the limits of legality to provide that aid where possible. Roosevelt agreed with the assessment of ADM Leahy and ADM Yarnell, who in 1937 contended that the allies in any future war the U.S. might face in the Far East "as indicated by...political and commercial considerations" would include Great Britain, France, and the Netherlands, that this list was "in order of natural affiliation as well as assured cooperation," and that "[a]s for pulling chestnuts out of the fire, England stands to pull just as many out for us as we do for her."[132]

---

[130] Edgar Dewitt Jones, President, The Federal Council of Churches of Christ in America, and Others, Letter to President Franklin Delano Roosevelt, 9 October 1937, in *Franklin D. Roosevelt and Foreign Affairs, January 1939-August 1939*, Donald B. Schewe, ed. (New York: Garland Publishing, Inc., 1979); Frederick J. Libby, Executive Secretary, National Council for Prevention of War, Washington, Letter to Representative Virginia E. Jenkes of Indiana, 28 September 1937, *Franklin D. Roosevelt and Foreign Affairs, January 1939-August 1939*, Donald B. Schewe, ed. (New York: Garland Publishing, Inc., 1979).

[131] Smith, *Ultra-Magic Deals*, 11-12; Reynolds, 55; Dorwart, *Conflict of Duty*, 113; James Leutze, "The Secret of the Churchill-Roosevelt Correspondence: September 1939-May 1940," *Journal of Contemporary History* 10, no. 3 (July 1975): 465.

[132] Harry E. Yarnell, ADM, USN, Commander in Chief, Asiatic Fleet, Letter to Admiral William D. Leahy, Chief of Naval Operations, 15 October 1937, in *Franklin D. Roosevelt and Foreign Affairs, January 1939-August 1939*, Donald B. Schewe, ed. (New York: Garland Publishing, Inc., 1979); Franklin D. Roosevelt, Letter to Admiral William D. Leahy, Chief of Naval Operations, 10 November 1937, in *Franklin D. Roosevelt and Foreign Affairs, January 1939-August 1939*, Donald B. Schewe, ed. (New York: Garland Publishing, Inc., 1979); William D. Leahy, Admiral, USN, Chief of Naval Operations, Letter to Franklin D. Roosevelt, 6 January 1938, in *Franklin D. Roosevelt and Foreign Affairs, December 1937-February 1938*, Donald B. Schewe, ed. (New York: Garland Publishing, Inc., 1979).

Roosevelt did what was possible to aid the British in the period before the war because maintaining British power would provide America the time it needed to rearm itself. Still, actions taken prior to his election in 1940, such as the institution of neutrality patrols, the resumption of the draft, and the destroyer-for-bases deal were all met with some public opposition in the U.S., which was why the staff talks and technical exchanges occurring between the U.S. and Great Britain were kept so secret. Although Roosevelt had greater freedom to act following his election, domestic politics still remained the great constraining factor on close relations between the two countries, a factor which would continue to cause tension between the U.S. and Great Britain up until the Pearl Harbor attack.[133]

Frank Knox

Confirmed in July of 1940 as Secretary of the Navy, Frank Knox has also been called an anglophile by some authors, although this assessment, just as with Roosevelt, understates the complexity of the situation.[134] Knox was a Republican and had been publisher of the Chicago Daily News, where he advocated an activist approach for American foreign policy as a necessary means of protecting U.S. national interests.[135] Knox was outraged that America had drawn down its military forces, as he believed that maintaining strength was the best way to maintain peace. Given this attitude, it is clear that Knox, although he admired the British, was not inclined to let them dictate American policy. He clearly desired a navy that was the "strongest in the world."[136] Like Roosevelt, he was a realist, as evidenced in a speech he made to the Cleveland Chamber of Commerce just after the start of the World War II. He made it clear that America really had nothing to fear from a British-French victory but "despite these pro-British and French sympathies, we must...think first of the interests of the United States, and what policy best serves those interests."[137] Later, as the Axis gained victory after victory on the Continent, Knox broadcast an impassioned plea for a more interventionist policy for America in a speech that warned the American people that "It Is Later Than You Think." In that address, he lamented an unprepared America and

---

[133] Dorwart, *Conflict of Duty*, 114; Smith, *Ultra-Magic Deals*, 8-9; Morison, *The Battle of the Atlantic*, 14-15, 33-34; Albion, 553-557; Reynolds, 64-65.

[134] Smith, *Ultra-Magic Deals*, 10-11.

[135] Frank Knox, Publisher, Chicago Daily News, Letter to Franklin D. Roosevelt, 15 December 1937, in *Franklin D. Roosevelt and Foreign Affairs, December 1937-February 1938*, ed. by Donald B. Schewe (New York: Garland Publishing, Inc., 1979).

[136] Frank Knox, Speech to Cleveland Chamber of Commerce, 24 October, 1939, in the *Papers of Frank Knox*, Operational Archives Branch, Naval Historical Center, Washington, D.C., 1-2. Cited hereafter as Knox, *Speech to Cleveland Chamber of Commerce*. Collection cited hereafter as Knox Papers.

[137] Frank Knox, *Speech to Cleveland Chamber of Commerce, Knox Papers*, 1-2.

praised the fighting spirit of the British, not because he was an anglophile, but for the most concrete of strategic reasons—"If she [England] falls, and her vast sea power is broken or seized...the Atlantic Ocean will cease to be our great barrier of defense."[138] For Knox, it was in America's self-interest to aid Great Britain and, while he may have felt an affinity for that country, it was his sound strategic sense which told him that America could not avoid war.

Admiral Harold R. Stark

ADM Stark relieved ADM Leahy as CNO on 1 August 1939. Stark was wary of the British most likely because, as ADM Sims' Flag Secretary, he had seen first-hand during World War I how the British treated their "junior partners," the Americans. Even though Stark had learned how to work with the British effectively, he, like many of his counterparts, was determined that the U.S. would only work with the British as equals in the future.[139] Despite a history of working successfully with the British, Stark's personal views show that he was unimpressed with them. In a personal letter to the commander of the U.S. Asiatic Squadron, Admiral T. C. Hart, Stark wrote that his Special Naval Observer (SPECNO) in London, RADM Ghormley, had just told him the British were expecting the U.S. to enter the war soon after Roosevelt's reelection in 1940. Stark told Hart this expectation on the part of the British was "merely another evidence of their slack ways of thought, and their non-realistic views of international political conditions, and of our own political system."[140]

Clearly, Stark was no fan of the British, yet, as the author of the famous "Plan Dog" memorandum in November 1940, he was responsible for "reversing the Pacific orientation [of U.S. military planning] and, in the midst of a national climate of independence and neutrality, proposed to enter a coalition war."[141] Once again, strategic imperatives led Stark to conclude, like his British counterparts, that alliance between the U.S. and the UK was necessary for the defeat of the Axis and the preservation of the democracies. The memo was written to Secretary of the Navy Knox, essentially as a plea to get definitive strategic direction from Roosevelt. Such strategic direction had become a necessity, given that RADM

---

[138] Frank Knox, "It Is Later Than You Think," 4 August 1940, in *Deadline for America, Knox Papers*, 2. In a speech given in January 1941, Knox said that those favoring the provision of aid to Great Britain should be called "A Committee to Aid Britain to *Aid Us* to Defend *America*." See Frank Knox, *Speech to the Canadian Society of New York*, 19 January 1941, *Knox Papers*, 11.

[139] Morison, *The Battle of the Atlantic*, 39; Department of the Navy, "Administrative History: United States Naval Forces in Europe 1940-1946," *Strategic Planning*, iv, cited hereafter as COMNAVEU Admin History; Budiansky, 52.

[140] Harold R. Stark, ADM, USN, Letter to ADM T.C. Hart, Commander-in-Chief, Asiatic Fleet, 12 Nov 40, *Stark Papers*, 1.

[141] Baer, 19.

Ghormley had sent word back from London that the British desired formal staff talks to discuss how U.S.-UK cooperation would work in the event the U.S. entered the war. To provide that direction, Stark and a team of planners that included his Deputy CNO, VADM Ingersoll, and his Director of War Plans, Rear Admiral Richmond Kelly Turner, drafted the 12-page memo over a 10-day period and submitted it to Knox, who forwarded it to Roosevelt for a decision.[142] While U.S. Army and Navy planners had focused attention on an Atlantic-first strategy as early as 1939 with the RAINBOW FIVE plan, most strategic planning up until that point had been oriented on Japan.[143] The situation in Europe had changed all that and Stark, despite his reservations about the British, clearly saw that America's future success was tied to an Atlantic-first strategy, which meant aiding the British. Setting out the parameters of the strategic problem which faced the U.S., Stark said "if Britain wins decisively against Germany we could win everywhere; but...if she loses the problem confronting us would be very great; and, while we might not *lose everywhere*, we might, possibly, not *win anywhere*."[144]

After outlining alternative courses of action, Stark persuasively argued why defense of Great Britain was in the U.S. national interest. Once again, displaying a mild disdain for the British, he stated that he felt "the British were over-optimistic as to their chances for ultimate success" and that success would require strong allies as "[a]lone the British Empire lacks the manpower and the material means to master Germany."[145] Citing the significant danger posed by the European situation, Stark forcefully recommended alliance with the British and explained how the focus of effort must first be victory in Europe with a holding action in the Far East.[146] To further this objective, Stark recommended that the U.S. military engage in "secret staff talks with the British military....to reach agreement and lay down plans for promoting unity of allied effort should the United States find it necessary to enter the war."[147] Roosevelt approved Stark's recommendation and the staff talks he recommended did occur. Stark's desire to aid Britain, like that of Roosevelt and Knox, was based on strategic realities rather than on pro-British attitudes. Still, just because Stark saw that aiding the British was in the best interests of the U.S., it was not a foregone conclusion that he would, by November 1940, overcome his suspicions concerning their motives enough to recommend engaging in secret staff talks with them. British actions from the summer of 1939

[142] Harold R. Stark, ADM, USN, Letter to Admiral J. O. Richardson, USN, Commander-in-Chief, U.S. Fleet, 12 November 1940, in *Stark Papers*.

[143] Baer, 18-19.

[144] Harold R. Stark, ADM, USN, Memorandum to Frank Knox, Secretary of the Navy, 12 November 1940, in *Stark Papers*, 1. Cited hereafter as *Plan Dog Memo*.

[145] Stark, *Plan Dog Memo, Stark Papers*, 4-5.

[146] Stark, *Plan Dog Memo, Stark Papers*, 23-24.

[147] Stark, *Plan Dog Memo, Stark Papers*, 26

through November of 1940 persuaded Stark that the British were serious about forming an equal partnership with the U.S., a factor that would encourage the Navy's leadership to authorize increased intelligence and technical exchanges with the British during this critical period.

Chapter 5

ALUSNA LONDON AND THE BRITISH NID
JANUARY 1939-MARCH 1941

The U.S. Navy Department's reactions to the Admiralty's initiatives in the field of intelligence cooperation were colored by domestic political considerations that precluded overt alliance and by vague feelings of disquiet that opening the cooperative door too far at this stage of the war might lead to a less than equal partnership later.

Alan Harris Bath, *Tracking the Axis Enemy*

Impact Of The War On Information Exchange

With regard to intelligence sharing, no relationship was more important or long standing than that which existed between the U.S. Naval Attaché office in London and the British NID. The London naval attaché office was the first the U.S. had established after the formation of ONI. While this office had numerous responsibilities, the most important relationship for the attaché to cultivate was the one maintained with the British DNI. Although a number of ad hoc forums for information exchange developed from 1939 to the early part of 1941, the British extensively used this particular, long-established conduit in their attempts to encourage greater cooperation between themselves and the Americans.

Figure 1. RADM Kirk

Source: ALUSNA London Command History," Stark Papers, v.

The U.S. Naval Attaché during this period, Captain Alan Goodrich Kirk (later RADM Kirk) was a key voice advocating for a more robust exchange of information between the U.S.

and Great Britain. His principal contact at the NID, Rear Admiral John Godfrey, was also an individual who did much to push for a more liberal exchange policy with the U.S. Kirk and Godfrey came from similar backgrounds and they were uniquely suited to perform the roles they were assigned at this critical juncture in U.S.-UK relations. The relationship they were able to establish, while not personally close, was a key component in furthering intelligence exchanges between the two countries.

Kirk's performance as attaché has been misrepresented by authors who contend that he was unrealistically pessimistic about England's chances of surviving the war.

Figure 2. RADM Godfrey

Source: Beesly, *Very Special Admiral*, contained in photo section, used by permission.

ALUSNA London Organization

Captain Alan Kirk took charge of the naval attaché office in London in February 1939. A highly capable surface warfare officer, VADM Kirk later commanded all U.S. naval forces engaged in the Normandy invasion. According to "insider" accounts, he was well respected and, despite his lack of intelligence training, performed his duties as attaché quite admirably.[148] The office he inherited from Captain Russell Willson consisted of three assistant naval attachés, three enlisted personnel, and four civil service employees. One officer was designated as liaison to the NID.[149] Although this organization was sufficient for handling peacetime operations, it was quickly overwhelmed within days of the war's commencement and, by mid-September 1939, Kirk began requesting additional personnel from

---

[148] Leutze, Bargaining for Supremacy, 58; Harold Stark, ADM, USN, Chief of Naval Operations, Letter to Robert Ghormley, RADM, USN, 16 November 1940, Stark Papers, 2.

[149] Department of the Navy, United States Naval Forces in Europe, "Office of the United States Naval Attaché American Embassy London England, 1939-1946," n.d., *Stark Papers*, 1-2. This document is the command history of ALUSNA London from 1939 to 1946. Cited hereafter as "ALUSNA London Command History," *Stark Papers*.

his immediate superior, the DNI, Rear Admiral Walter S. Anderson, who honored this and future requests. By December 1940 the attaché office had expanded to 30 officers, in addition to numerous "naval observers" who would be assigned to England temporarily on specific fact-finding missions.[150] This significant increase in personnel was needed to handle the ever-increasing flow of information and intelligence provided by the British as the war progressed. The path to establishing the U.S. naval observers with the British military and scientific establishments was not an easy one as mutual distrust hampered the flow of information between the two countries well into 1940.

The Boom Defense-Arresting Gear Deal

Despite direction from his superior to engage in greater information exchange with the British, CAPT Willson had been stymied in his efforts to obtain more information. The main problem was the fact that neither the British nor the Americans were willing to give up the technical secrets that the other side wanted. Prior to Willson's departure, agreement was reached that the U.S. and the UK would explore the possibility of exchanging information on the British harbor boom defenses for details of the arresting gear used aboard U.S. naval carriers. At least one author has characterized this exchange as minor.[151] While it may appear so, it was, in fact, significant to both countries at the time and this event clearly shows the limits of the possible, with regard to information exchange, in the period prior to the start of the war.

While Willson and Godfrey had laid the ground work for this exchange prior to Willson's departure in February 1939, it was June of that year before Kirk could provide Godfrey with a timeline in which the exchange would take place. Kirk informed Godfrey that he should look to send his observer to the U.S. sometime in July or August of 1939, which disappointed Godfrey, given that this was nearly eight months after the exchange had been agreed to.[152] The contrast between the two countries' approaches to these exchanges is interesting, as they began just two weeks before the war started. In the matter of the exchange of boom defense information, Captain H. E. Fischer and Commander G. W. Nelson were cordially

---

[150] Alan Goodrich Kirk, CAPT, USN, Letter to Rear Admiral Walter S. Anderson, USN, Director of Naval Intelligence, 15 September 1939, *Kirk Papers*; Walter S. Anderson, RADM, USN, Director of Naval Intelligence, Letter to Captain Alan Goodrich Kirk, USN, 20 September 1939, Kirk Papers, n.p; "ALUSNA London Command History," *Stark Papers*, 2.

[151] Zimmerman, 32-33.

[152] Alan Goodrich Kirk, CAPT, USN, Letter to Rear Admiral Walter S. Anderson, USN, Director of Naval Intelligence, 28 June 1939, *Kirk Papers*. Then-CNO ADM Leahy actually approved the exchange on 27 July 1939. For additional information see William Leahy, ADM, USN, Chief of Naval Operations, Memorandum to the Chiefs of the Bureaus of Ordnance, Construction and Repair, and Yards and Docks, 27 July 1939, *DNI Correspondence*.

received by the British and from the start of their visit Kirk was able to report that they were receiving full cooperation from their hosts and were even allowed to inspect the British anchorage at Scapa Flow to see the boom defenses in operation. In all, Fischer and Nelson were in England for well over a month and they were able to say with confidence that they had "gotten just about everything worthwhile on the subject of boom defenses" from their British hosts.[153]

The British sent Royal Navy Captain R. M. Ellis to the *USS Saratoga* to learn what he could about the American arresting gear. Officers aboard the *Saratoga* were given clear instructions that they were not to provide any details of aircraft characteristics to the Royal Navy officer, but they could discuss other matters of a non-sensitive nature. Ellis impressed the U.S. officers he came in contact with, especially the Commander of Carrier Division ONE, Rear Admiral William "Bull" Halsey, who admired Ellis' confidence in the Royal Air Force and his willingness to discuss British aviation.[154] Even though the exchange went well and American officers were impressed with British openness, there was still tremendous reticence on the part of the Navy hierarchy to share anything beyond what had been so arduously agreed to. For example, Ellis had asked questions about night carrier landings and barrier crash rates, but he had been rebuffed onboard the *Saratoga*. Efforts by the British Assistant Naval Attaché to obtain this information were also denied.[155] Even Kirk tried to capitalize on the momentum he had hoped this exchange would generate by trying to convince Anderson that the British should, at the very least, be given details on the Navy's aircraft cast recovery system since, now that they were exposed to it from Ellis' visit, they would quickly figure out how to replicate it on their own.[156] As with the information requested by the British, Anderson was forced to tell Kirk that the details of the system would need to remain confidential.[157]

---

[153] Alan Goodrich Kirk, CAPT, USN, Letter to Rear Admiral Walter S. Anderson, USN, Director of Naval Intelligence, 14 August 1939, *Kirk Papers*; H. E. Fischer, CAPT, USN, Letter to U.S. Naval Attaché, London (Captain Alan G. Kirk), 23 September 1939, *DNI Correspondence*.

[154] Chief of Bureau of Aeronautics (Rear Admiral J. H. Towers, USN), Letter to the Chief of Naval Operations, 15 July 1939, *DNI Correspondence*; Commander Carrier Division ONE (Rear Admiral W. H. Halsey), Letter to Director of Naval Intelligence (Rear Admiral Walter S. Anderson), 14 August 1939.

[155] Commanding Officer, U.S. Fleet, Aircraft Battle Force, Letter to Director of Naval Intelligence (Rear Admiral Walter S. Anderson), 12 August 1939, *DNI Correspondence*; F. J. A. Coleby, CDR, Royal Navy, Letter to Director of Naval Intelligence (Rear Admiral Walter S. Anderson), 22 August 1939, *DNI Correspondence*.

[156] Alan Goodrich Kirk, CAPT, USN, Letter to Rear Admiral Walter S. Anderson, USN, Director of Naval Intelligence, 19 August 1939, *DNI Correspondence*.

[157] Walter S. Anderson, RADM, USN, Director of Naval Intelligence, Letter to Captain Alan Goodrich Kirk, USN, 5 September 1939, *DNI Correspondence*.

While the boom defense-arresting gear deal showed the limits of the exchanges between the two navies on the eve of the war, the situation would begin to change substantially once the war began. For example, a week after the war began, the British Naval Attaché, CAPT Curzon-Howe, requested details from the U.S. on its HF/DF network, stating the British were prepared to exchange full details of their network in exchange.[158] Anderson agreed to this exchange, although he made it clear that the U.S. was not prepared to exchange the intelligence derived from this source to the British, but rather merely the structure of the network.[159]

British Attitudes on Intelligence Exchange
September 1939 to May 1940

Despite the qualified success of the boom defense-arresting gear deal, the commencement of the war in September 1939 would make the sharing of intelligence more difficult. As Patrick Beesly has noted, "[f]or the first six months of the war both sides were anxious to receive but loath to give" information to the other side.[160] With respect to the British, many authors have cited security concerns as the main reason for their reluctance to share intelligence.[161] The archival data clearly show that security was the main British concern and that it had a significant impact on intelligence cooperation during the first months of the war. When reflecting on this period, CAPT Kirk remembered that obtaining information on the new German magnetic mine was a primary intelligence objective of his office. The British were reluctant to tell the U.S. anything about the mine during the first month of the war "because they didn't think our security in Washington was good enough to prevent the Germans finding out what they knew."[162] Kirk's letters to his superiors during this period also reflect his growing frustration with the British. In January of 1940, he and his men had considerable difficulty getting anything from the Admiralty and they were told, in confidence, that porous U.S. security was the reason. When Kirk confronted Godfrey with this problem, he was shown an article in the Army & Navy *Register* that clearly indicated monies allocated for harbor defenses were to purchase netting and other

---

[158] L. Curzon-Howe, CAPT, Royal Navy, Naval Attaché, Letter to Rear Admiral Walter S. Anderson, USN, Director of Naval Intelligence, 8 September 1939, *DNI Correspondence*.

[159] Walter S. Anderson, RADM, USN, Director of Naval Intelligence, Letter to Captain L. Curzon-Howe, M.V.O., Royal Navy, Naval Attaché, 25 September 1939, *DNI Correspondence*. The first exchange occurred in the spring of 1940 when two U.S. Navy personnel visited the British HF/DF site at Bermuda where they observed "British operations, net procedures, and the employment of fixed antenna equipment." For additional information see Bray, xviii.

[160] Beesly, *Very Special Admiral*, 174.

[161] Zimmerman, 47-48; Leutze, "Technology and Bargaining," 54.

[162] *Kirk Reminiscences*, 143.

gear designed by the British. Although this was the only leak Godfrey could point to, Kirk noted that the widespread perception of lax U.S. security would be difficult to overcome.[163]

Kirk acknowledged to his superiors that the British attitude toward U.S. security was not universal. In February 1940 he had a long conversation with Godfrey, one of the few extended conversations he had had with the DNI since the start of the war. In that conversation, Kirk appealed to Godfrey to provide more information to the U.S. because it would be in the best interests of the British to have an America prepared for war. Godfrey confidentially told Kirk that he had been advocating increased sharing of information within his own government, because he also believed it to be in Britain's long term interest to have America prepared. Godfrey, however, was hamstrung by the policies of the Royal Navy's technical divisions, which did not favor sharing information with the Americans, even though they could point to no concrete evidence of U.S. security lapses. Kirk felt Godfrey was sincere and recommended to his superiors that one way to break the logjam would be for the U.S. to more expeditiously provide requested information and intelligence to the British, a policy Godfrey advised him would be most helpful for fostering cooperation. Kirk made it clear to Godfrey, though, that 1940 was an election year in the U.S. and domestic political concerns significantly impacted the amount of cooperation the U.S. could provide.[164]

As late as April 1940, despite the fact the British had begun to provide the U.S. with more intelligence, Kirk was still dissatisfied with the amount and pace of exchange between the two countries and he confronted Godfrey about the problem. The report Kirk wrote following that conversation was significant, as it pointed to other concerns the British had with regard to the sharing of information, concerns having little to do with security. Although Kirk was aware that Godfrey was personally doing what he could to provide more information to the Americans, he intentionally prodded Godfrey, who had just complimented the U.S. on the decision to redeploy its fleet to Hawaii, by telling him that the fleet would be a lot better prepared if the U.S. had the secret of degaussing.[165] Godfrey was incensed and the tirade he unleashed on Kirk is worth quoting at some length

---

[163] Alan Goodrich Kirk, CAPT, USN, Letter to Rear Admiral Walter S. Anderson, USN, Director of Naval Intelligence, 22 January 1940, *Kirk Papers*, 1-2.

[164] Alan Goodrich Kirk, CAPT, USN, Letter to Rear Admiral Walter S. Anderson, USN, Director of Naval Intelligence, 6 February, 1940, *Kirk Papers*, 1-3.

[165] Alan Goodrich Kirk, CAPT, USN, Letter to Rear Admiral Walter S. Anderson, USN, Director of Naval Intelligence, 24 April 1940, *Kirk Papers*, 1. Cited hereafter as Kirk, Letter to Anderson, 24 April 1940. Degaussing refers to the process of reducing a ship's magnetic signature through the use of electrically charged coils embedded within the ship's hull.

because it illustrates the larger geopolitical concerns that motivated British hesitancy to share information at this stage in the war. Godfrey told Kirk

> that he felt they had done a great deal for us. He cited the visits to the damaged ships, as well as the magnetic mine. He said he was constantly being told by people to whom he referred matters in which I [Kirk] was interested that the United States wasn't in the war, and insisted she was never coming into the war, so that various Divisions of the Naval Staff...were intimating that, after all, why should they give the American Navy information which they were earning with their own blood and sweat. He also made reference to the fact that if all this material was furnished now; then, during the period of peace, say, 25 years or more which they hoped would follow this war, we would be abreast of them throughout.[166]

Godfrey thus revealed that resentment of the U.S. for not entering the war, and British concerns that the U.S. would later use the information provided to them to eclipse Great Britain, were two other significant factors in the mind of the Admiralty's officers which prevented wider exchange of information.[167]

Kirk was sobered by Godfrey's remarks and told DNI Anderson that Godfrey's concerns were legitimate. He explained how the British had requested information on stern hangers, airdropped depth charges, underwater paint, and the latest American naval exercise (Fleet Problem XXI), but that none of these requests had been honored. Despite these tensions, by this time Kirk felt that he was receiving more from the British than he had in the past and saw the relationship, which seemed so badly fractured in December 1939, as improving. He reiterated to his superiors that the U.S. needed to reciprocate with their own exchanges because the British had much to share and the U.S. could not long expect "to get something for nothing."[168]

---

[166] Kirk, Letter to Anderson, 24 April 1940, 2.

[167] For additional information on British concerns about their declining position relative to the U.S. and their fears of what cooperation with the U.S. might mean for the future of the Empire in the post-war world, see Reynolds, 10, 15; Aldrich, xiv.

[168] Kirk, Letter to Anderson, 24 April 1940, 2-3. Years later, Kirk would recall this time period accurately, telling the interviewer who assisted him with his reminiscences that, while the exchange of information was not "wide-open," the British were far more willing to share than were the Americans. For additional information see *Kirk Reminiscences*, 133.

American Attitudes On Intelligence Exchange
September 1939 to May 1940

Since Kirk and Godfrey both observed that the exchange of information during this period appeared somewhat one-sided, what were the American reasons for restricting the flow of information to the British at this juncture? British refusals to share information during the chaotic first few months of the war suggested to some personnel in the U.S. Navy that the British were untrustworthy and capricious, and they were disinclined to honor British requests for information because of this attitude.[169] Domestic political concerns, continually a constraint on U.S. foreign policy moves, were also a factor that weighed heavily against getting too close to the British. Despite the rebuffs, Kirk continued to press for something he could give the British in exchange for what they had shared with the U.S. Navy. Even something as simple as getting a British officer permission to observe Fleet Problem XXI was impossible. When asked about why the Navy could not accede to this request, considering the fact the British had allowed U.S. Naval Officers to observe some of their operations, Anderson told Kirk that there was nothing he could do about it and, while he could not elaborate, the refusal "was made by higher authority" and he agreed with the decision.[170] The most likely explanation for the refusal, given Anderson's cryptic rationale, were domestic political concerns, as the media and Congress were vigilant for any signs the administration was moving the country in a direction that would embroil it in another war. The risk was too high that news of a British observer with the U.S. fleet would leak, which would be costly to both President Roosevelt and the Navy Department in terms of public good will and Congressional support.

While Kirk acknowledged that Anderson had a bigger picture of the situation than he did, he thought the U.S. was missing a golden opportunity by not reciprocating with them as war was causing the British to make rapid technological advances.[171] Kirk found it hard to comprehend why his superiors could not see why "it appears so simply to our advantage to open up with them [the British]...that it is a puzzle to me...to appreciate the factors which appear to weigh so heavily against such a policy."[172] Despite his admiration for how the war was

---

[169] Leutze, "Technology and Bargaining," 54-55.

[170] Walter S. Anderson, RADM, USN, Director of Naval Intelligence, Letter to Captain Alan Goodrich Kirk, USN, 1 April 1940, *Kirk Papers*.

[171] Alan Goodrich Kirk, CAPT, USN, Letter to Rear Admiral Walter S. Anderson, USN, Director of Naval Intelligence, n.d., *Kirk Papers*. This was a handwritten note attached to Kirk, Letter to Anderson, 24 April 1940. Since it seems to respond to the views Anderson expressed in his 1 April 1940 letter to Kirk, cited directly above, it is likely he added the note as a postscript to his 24 April 1940 correspondence after receiving Anderson's 1 April 1940 letter.

[172] Kirk, Letter to Anderson, 24 April 1940, 4.

accelerating British capabilities, however, Kirk did fall prey to technical chauvinism. While believing the British were probably farther along than the Americans in anti-submarine warfare and harbor defenses, he also believed that the U.S. was "pretty far ahead of [the British] in certain things [like]...air operations" and anti-air defenses.[173] Technical chauvinism would play a major role in U.S. resistance to engage in technical exchanges with the British, as many naval officers felt the U.S. was on the cutting edge of technology in all fields and had little to gain from sharing their superior advances with the British.

Initial Steps Toward Improved Cooperation
— The Kirk-Godfrey Relationship

Bridging the Divide—British Cultivation of the U.S. Naval Attaché

Godfrey, along with others in British intelligence, firmly believed it was in the best interests of the British to provide information to the Americans without the expectation of getting any short-term benefits from the exchange. Although a relatively low-level figure in the policy realm, as DNI Godfrey had the ear of the Royal Navy's leadership and, through them, to Prime Minister Neville Chamberlain and Churchill. His admirers have credited him with having a key role in the development of the U.S.-UK alliance, saying that Godfrey saw from the outset "that the British goal must be to draw the Americans closer and closer and that this could best be achieved by providing them with as much information as possible."[174] At the start of the war, Godfrey's main conduit for his attempt to influence U.S. policy was the U.S. naval attaché, Kirk. Most authors have concluded that Godfrey cultivated Kirk, providing him what information he could to earn U.S. goodwill and that he, personally, did not care about the lack of equitable information exchange.[175] For Godfrey, the long-term benefit was the addition of U.S. strength to the British cause.

The observation that Godfrey cultivated Kirk leaves the misimpression that Kirk's advocacy for greater information exchange with the British was based entirely on Godfrey's influence. However, while Godfrey's willingness to provide

---

[173] Kirk, Letter to Anderson, 24 April 1940, 3-4. Presumably, Kirk's reference to America's advanced anti-air defense capabilities was a reference to the U.S.'s nascent radar capability, an area where the British were actually far ahead of the Americans. Interestingly, James Leutze speculates that Godfrey assumed the U.S. reluctance to engage in technical exchanges was based on embarrassment rooted in American technical inferiority, an indication that technical chauvinism cut both ways. For additional information see Leutze, "Technology and Bargaining," 54; Zimmerman, 28-29.

[174] Beesly, *Very Special Admiral*, 173. For additional information see MacLachlan, 216-29; Leutze, "Technology and Bargaining," 51, Dorwart, *Conflict of Duty*, 140-141.

[175] Dorwart, *Conflict of Duty*, 140; MacLachlan, 216.

information did have an impact on Kirk, his desire to reciprocate these exchanges was based on his fear that, if the U.S. did not reciprocate, the British would eventually cut him off completely. Kirk's repeated calls for a more liberal exchange policy on the part of the U.S. Navy were based on his assessment "that as the British Navy gains in war experience they will gradually outdistance us in many technical subjects. It has seemed to me [to] our benefit, on the whole, to seize any opportunity for making exchanges."[176] Kirk, like Godfrey, saw that the U.S. would one day fight in the war and, when that happened, America would be on the British side. War was, for Kirk, the great laboratory, and cutting off access to that source of information for short-term political interests was a policy Kirk did not agree with, although he assured his superiors that he would stand by their decisions as they had the broader view of the situation.[177]

NID Information Exchange with the U.S. Naval Attaché

Developments from June 1939 through May 1940 demonstrate that Godfrey did use information as a tool to forge a closer bond with Kirk, hoping this would result in closer cooperation between the two governments. At their first meeting, Godfrey told Kirk that he "would be free to see him at any time on any subject" and Kirk felt that a close liaison could be established because the British wanted "to keep in close touch with an eye on eventualities."[178] Soon after this visit, Godfrey took Kirk to the basement of the Admiralty where he was shown the plot room and country desks. Although he was not allowed into some of the rooms, such as the Code and Signal Room, he was shown the communications center and was given a briefing on the British HF/DF stations and the associated equipment used to obtain crossfixes.[179] During this same period, Godfrey also provided Kirk some strategic intelligence regarding German war preparations; namely, by sharing a report that the DNI expected the war would begin by mid-August. He also

---

[176] Alan Goodrich Kirk, CAPT, USN, Letter to Rear Admiral Walter S. Anderson, USN, Director of Naval Intelligence, 3 November 1939, *Kirk Papers*, 1. Cited hereafter as Kirk, Letter to Anderson, 3 November 1939. In addition to the references cited above where Kirk advocates for closer exchange with the British see also Alan Goodrich Kirk, CAPT, USN, Letter to Rear Admiral Walter S. Anderson, USN, Director of Naval Intelligence, 5 January 1940, *Kirk Papers*, 1.

[177] Kirk, Letter to Anderson, 3 November 1939, 1.

[178] Alan Goodrich Kirk, CAPT, USN, Letter to Rear Admiral Walter S. Anderson, USN, Director of Naval Intelligence, 20 June 1939, *Kirk Papers*, 1-2.

[179] Alan Goodrich Kirk, CAPT, USN, Letter to Rear Admiral Walter S. Anderson, USN, Director of Naval Intelligence, 28 June 1939, *Kirk Papers*, 1. The Admiralty's Operational Intelligence Center would not officially stand up until August 1939, though the arrangement Kirk describes is very similar to the setup for the OIC described by Patrick Beesly. For additional information see Beesly, *Very Special Intelligence*, 19-23.

gave Kirk information on six German U-boats operating in the Atlantic.[180] From Kirk's comments to Anderson, it was obvious that Kirk had formed a favorable impression of British naval intelligence efforts.

While British reluctance to share intelligence once war broke out in September 1939 can be attributed to the factors cited above, there were more mundane problems that militated against the exchange of information in the first few months of the war. Kirk reported that factors such as logistics, lack of social opportunities, and the movement of some Admiralty offices during the

Figure 3. German Propaganda on Kirk's Visit.

Source: Alan Goodrich Kirk, CAPT, USN, Letter to RADM Walter S. Anderson, 20 November 1939, *Kirk Papers.*

first few months of the war significantly hindered the flow of information.[181] Despite the restrictions, Kirk was able to gather some information and his small staff began 24-hour operations in the first few weeks of the war. In October 1939, Godfrey told Kirk that he had permission to visit the Home Fleet, at Thurso in Northern Scotland, leaving Kirk with the impression he could stay there a few days to observe fleet defenses. Kirk only stayed one night, however, when he learned that the Commander of the British Fleet, ADM Forbes, while receiving him cordially, had not been informed of the purpose of his visit. In actuality, Winston Churchill had directed Godfrey to send Kirk to Thurso as part of a plan by the British to counter German propaganda. The Germans claimed they had sunk the *Ark Royal* and Kirk was able to verify that the British aircraft carrier was in excellent condition on his return to London.[182] Kirk's visit became fodder for the Nazi propagandists (see cartoon). In his letter forwarding this graphic to Anderson, Kirk displays no rancor at having been used by the British, in fact, he seemed to relish the role he played in

---

[180] Alan Goodrich Kirk, CAPT, USN, Letter to Rear Admiral Walter S. Anderson, USN, Director of Naval Intelligence, 28 June 1939, Kirk Papers, 1-3. This was the second letter to Anderson dated 28 June 1939.

[181] "ALUSNA London Command History," *Stark Papers, 3.*

[182] Alan Goodrich Kirk, CAPT, USN, Letter to Rear Admiral Walter S. Anderson, USN, Director of Naval Intelligence, 10 October 1939, *Kirk Papers*, 1-2.

the affair.[183] This lack of resentment likely had more to do with Kirk's anti-Nazi feelings than his pro-British tendencies. Like most officers of his generation, Kirk remained wary of the British, as evidenced when he forwarded a detailed intelligence report on Mexico to Anderson that Godfrey had provided him in November 1939. Kirk asked Anderson to have ONI's analysts take a hard look at it and to let him know if the information in it could be confirmed. As he told Anderson, "[i]t would help me to know whether or not I am being made a 'stooge.'"[184] Kirk's concerns demonstrate that, although he was receptive to Godfrey's overtures, he was not blindly trustful of what the DNI provided him.

The two most significant items of information the British gave Kirk during this period, items given without any reciprocal exchange from the U.S., as Godfrey pointed out, were intelligence on the German magnetic mine and the opportunity to examine vessels damaged in enemy action. The decision to give the Americans the information on the mine was very significant, given British security concerns, but the Admiralty reasoned that one day the American Navy would join their fight, and if the U.S. fleet was vulnerable to this type of mine it would be an ineffective force until such time as they could install the proper countermeasures.[185] In early November 1939, Kirk was invited to the Admiralty to speak to the Director of the Minesweeping Division, CAPT Morse, who told Kirk the information he was going to give him needed to "be treated with the utmost secrecy" as the British government was very concerned the Germans would find out just how effective the mine had been.[186] While the British had not recovered a mine intact at this point, they shared every bit of data they had with Kirk, to include their theories on the actuation method, size of the explosive payload, the method of delivery, the most effective deployment depth of the mine, its destructive effect, and how the British were attempting to counter it using an experimental degaussing method.[187] Kirk was also given information about the German 21-inch torpedo, the British asdic system (sonar), and he was notified by the British

---

[183] Alan Goodrich Kirk, CAPT, USN, Letter to Rear Admiral Walter S. Anderson, USN, Director of Naval Intelligence, 20 November 1939, *Kirk Papers*, 1.

[184] Alan Goodrich Kirk, CAPT, USN, Letter to Rear Admiral Walter S. Anderson, USN, Director of Naval Intelligence, 9 November 1939, *Kirk Papers*.

[185] Leutze, "Technology and Bargaining," 56.

[186] Alan Goodrich Kirk, CAPT, USN, Letter to Rear Admiral Walter S. Anderson, USN, Director of Naval Intelligence, Enclosure (B) to letter dated 6 November 1939, *Kirk Papers*, 1. Cited hereafter as Kirk, Enclosure (B) to Letter to Anderson, 6 November 1939.

[187] Kirk, Enclosure (B) to Letter to Anderson, 6 November 1939, 1-4.

when they had recovered a magnetic mine in late November.[188] The British continued to update Kirk on the progress of their exploitation of the mine and provided him details on the experimental countermeasure techniques they were using to counter it. Clearly, British openness on this important matter was beginning to have an impact on Kirk, as he had taken to referring to CAPT Morse as "his friend" in correspondence.[189] As shown above, it was after the New Year when Kirk became very forceful in his letters to Anderson concerning the need to reciprocate to keep the valuable stream of information coming. While Kirk's motivations may have been different from what Godfrey hoped they would be, as there are few expressions of sympathy for the British situation in Kirk's correspondence, the Admiralty's openness was having the desired effect on Kirk, who was vociferously advocating more cooperation between the two countries.

For Kirk, the most significant breakthrough in the British attitude on exchanges came in March 1940. At that time, Godfrey told Kirk that the British were in the process of forming a committee that would look into the matter of exchanges and asked Kirk to come up with a list of U.S. information requirements. What Godfrey was alluding to was the British technical exchange mission that would be led by one of England's leading scientists, Dr. Henry Tizard. The Tizard mission, discussed in the next chapter, would have a profound and positive effect on the cooperation the U.S. would give the British in the matter of informa-

---

[188] Alan Goodrich Kirk, CAPT, USN, Letter to Rear Admiral Walter S. Anderson, USN, Director of Naval Intelligence, Enclosure (A) to letter dated 6 November 1939, *Kirk Papers*, 1-2; Alan Goodrich Kirk, CAPT, USN, Letter to Rear Admiral Walter S. Anderson, USN, Director of Naval Intelligence, 24 November 1939, *Kirk Papers*, 1-2; Alan Goodrich Kirk, CAPT, USN, Letter to Rear Admiral Walter S. Anderson, USN, Director of Naval Intelligence, 9 November 1939, *Kirk Papers*. Interestingly, the offer to provide the U.S. information on asdic originated from Churchill, who offered the technology as part of his campaign to entice Roosevelt into a closer relationship with the UK. In the preceding reference (Kirk's 9 November 1939 letter to Anderson) Kirk remarks that Godfrey was caught off guard when Kirk raised the subject of exchange of information on asdic, apparently unaware that Churchill had made the offer, which had filtered down from Roosevelt through the U.S. Navy Department to Kirk. The details of the exchange of asdic technology would take many months to conclude. For additional information see Zimmerman, 43-46; Alan Goodrich Kirk, CAPT, USN, Letter to Rear Admiral Walter S. Anderson, USN, Director of Naval Intelligence, 14 March 1940, *Kirk Papers*; James Leutze, "The Secret of the Churchill-Roosevelt Correspondence: September 1939-May 1940," *Journal of Contemporary History* 10, no. 3 (July 1975), 472, cited hereafter as Leutze, "Secret Churchill-Roosevelt Correspondence."

[189] Alan Goodrich Kirk, CAPT, USN, Letter to Rear Admiral Walter S. Anderson, USN, Director of Naval Intelligence, 6 December 1939, *Kirk Papers*, 1-2. Although Kirk never formed a close personal relationship with Godfrey, he would fondly recall that he became good friends with ADM Fraser, the Admiralty's comptroller, and CAPT Miles, the Admiralty's Director of Ordnance. For additional information see *Kirk Reminiscences*, 144-145.

tion exchanges. Even more significant for Kirk, he was informed by Godfrey that the Admiralty would now allow personnel from the U.S. naval attaché office to inspect damaged British ships in dry-dock. Kirk was ecstatic at this opportunity and quickly dispatched his assistant naval attachés to Bath where they could inspect ships damaged during a recent German attack on Scapa Flow. This privilege was exclusive to the American attachés and Kirk was full of praise for the openness that the British displayed in giving his personnel virtually unrestricted access to the damaged vessels and answering any enquires his men had.[190]

Also in March 1940, Kirk met with the British comptroller, ADM Fraser, who requested information on stern hangers and aircraft-dropped depth charges in exchange for access to the British ships. But ADM Fraser also told Kirk that it was the "1st Sea Lord's express wish—that we should not be perpetually 'bargaining', but if, on a 'goodwill' basis we could give them an occasional lead...they, for their part, were very glad to be helpful."[191] Here was both the promise and the implied threat to Kirk, that greater cooperation would reap even more information from the British, but continued reluctance on the part of the Americans to honor any requests would make it difficult for the British to continue giving the Americans such preferential treatment. British concerns in this area were understandable. Even though it appears the Americans were still passing information on Japanese naval movements to the British, as agreed to during the Ingersoll Mission in 1938, there is little evidence to indicate what else the U.S. was providing during this period.[192] Given Godfrey's display of pique, noted above, and Kirk's repeated pleas to Anderson for more openness, we can deduce that the U.S. gave very little.[193]

---

[190] Alan Goodrich Kirk, CAPT, USN, Letter to Rear Admiral Walter S. Anderson, USN, Director of Naval Intelligence, 21 March 1940, *Kirk Papers*, 1-2; Alan Goodrich Kirk, CAPT, USN, Letter to Rear Admiral Walter S. Anderson, USN, Director of Naval Intelligence, 26 March 1940, *Kirk Papers*, 1-3; Alan Goodrich Kirk, CAPT, USN, Letter to Rear Admiral Walter S. Anderson, USN, Director of Naval Intelligence, 29 March 1940, *Kirk Papers*, 1; Alan Goodrich Kirk, CAPT, USN, Letter to Rear Admiral Walter S. Anderson, USN, Director of Naval Intelligence, 3 April 1940, *Kirk Papers*, 1-2.

[191] Alan Goodrich Kirk, CAPT, USN, Letter to Rear Admiral Walter S. Anderson, USN, Director of Naval Intelligence, 21 March 1940, *Kirk Papers*, 3. This was one of the information requests Godfrey was referring to when he castigated Kirk for the lack of information exchange reciprocity on the part of the Americans.

[192] Bath, 25; Leutze, "Secret Churchill-Roosevelt Correspondence," 484.

[193] Even when requests made by the British were honored, mistakes were made. The U.S. Navy did eventually get around to providing the British information on airdropped depth charges, a request first made in Fall 1939, but they did not do so until April 1940. To make matters worse, the Navy Department provided the information to the British Air Attaché, Group-Captain George Pirie, rather than to the British Naval Attaché, CAPT Curzon-Howe, this even though it was the Royal Navy which had repeatedly made the request. Kirk advised Anderson to provide the information to Curzon-Howe. For additional information see Alan Goodrich Kirk, CAPT, USN, Letter to Rear Admiral Walter S. Anderson, USN, Director of Naval Intelligence, 2 May 1940, *Kirk Papers*, 1-2.

Chapter 6

COURTING THE RELUCTANT ALLY
JUNE 1940-MARCH 1941

From the standpoint of naval policy-making in the external field, the 27 months of World War II before Pearl Harbor rank in significance with the succeeding 45 months during which the United States was a formal belligerent. By the time of the Japanese sneak attack, the major pattern of strategic effort had already been hammered out in close conjunction with the British.

Robert Greenhalgh Albion, *Makers of naval policy, 1798-1947*

British Maneuvers

From the summer of 1940 through the spring of 1941, secret development of the cooperative relationship between America and Great Britain took place on many levels. While the leadership of the U.S. and its navy were predisposed to aid the British, this predisposition was based on a realistic appraisal of U.S. national interests rather than on favoritism. Mutual distrust was a factor both countries would need to contend with and, despite the many channels of communication that developed between the two countries, attitudes and assumptions would continue to bring miscues that resulted in numerous faltering steps toward alliance. Still, by March 1941, with the completion of the American-British-Canadian Staff Talks (ABC-1), the U.S. and the UK had essentially completed their strategic rapprochement. By then, the depth and breadth of intelligence exchange occurring between the two countries were several times greater than anything either country would have envisioned when the war began in September 1939. With but one important exception, all of the major forums designed to improve cooperation between the two countries were the result of British initiatives. Many of the initiatives occurred concurrently.

William Stephenson and British Security Coordination

Even as many of the initiatives the British took to entice America into cooperating with their war effort were overt, one long-running covert component actively attempted to influence U.S. decisionmakers into entering the war on the side of Great Britain. Much of this story has been told elsewhere. A complete, although unofficial, accounting of British overt and covert intelligence activities in America, written just after the war by members of the British Security Coordination (BSC) mission, is now available for scholarly evaluation.[194] Historians have assessed the BSC report and found it largely consistent with available the historical data.[195]

Rhodri Jeffreys-Jones observes that the main purpose of the BSC was not to provide the U.S. with intelligence "but to persuade the United States, by trickery if necessary, to enter the war and to do so on the side of the Allies."[196] To accomplish this purpose, Churchill sent retired Army Colonel William Stephenson, a Canadian millionaire, to take over the British Passport Control Officer (PCO) post in New York City, to replace Sir James Paget. The PCO was the thinly veiled cover for the senior SIS officer in the United States and the role of this office was known to high-ranking officials in the U.S. government.[197] While Stephenson's primary point of contact for counterintelligence and counterespionage activities in the U.S. was FBI Director J. Edgar Hoover, he was also in personal contact with Roosevelt, both directly and through associates like Vincent Astor, and he had good relations with the Secretaries of State, War, and the Navy.[198] Stephenson's first move on taking over the office was to create an "umbrella organization" for British covert activities in North America, renaming his organization British Security Coordination (BSC), at Hoover's suggestion, and gathering together operatives from MI5, SIS, and SOE operating in America under his control. The organization was divided into four branches—the Secret Intelligence Division, the Security Branch, Special Operations, and Propaganda. Although relations between the old PCO office and the FBI had been strained in previous years, Stephenson was able to mend fences with Hoover and received approval from Roosevelt for his office to act as the MI5 and SIS liaison in America. Conscious of the strict neutrality laws and State Department sensitivities over any moves toward closer cooperation with Great Britain, Stephenson's direct liaison on intelligence matters was initially limited to Hoover himself, to maintain the secrecy of the British mission.[199]

---

[194] *British Security Coordination: The Secret History of British Intelligence in the Americas, 1940-1945* (New York: Fromm International, 1999).

[195] For additional information see Thomas Mahl, *Desperate Deception: British Covert Operations in the United States, 1939-1944* (Washington, DC: Brassey's Inc., 1998). Mahl provides an excellent summary of the BSC report and focuses his study on the British attempts to covertly influence U.S. public opinion, through co-opted media outlets and reporters, and their attempts to influence U.S. political elections by targeting isolationist politicians for defeat.

[196] Jeffreys-Jones, 8.

[197] BSC, *Secret History*, ix; Bath, 12-13.

[198] Dorwart, *Conflict of Duty*, 142; Hinsley, *British Intel* vol. 1, 312-313; BSC, *Secret History*, xxxvi, 5, 8, 17.

[199] BSC, ix-x; xxv-xxvi.

The officially declared mission of the BSC was to act as liaison between U.S. and British security services, ostensibly to protect British war supplies flowing from America.[200] To this end, the Security Division oversaw industrial and transportation security issues and became actively involved in exchanging information on suspected saboteurs and subversives with the FBI, the MID, and ONI, assisting those organizations in their counterintelligence and security functions.[201] Cooperation with Hoover was especially important during the first year of the BSC's existence as both the War and Navy departments were wary of coordinating with the British on anything other than security arrangements, lest they violate the intent of the neutrality laws. Hoover enjoyed this special relationship with Stephenson as it allowed him to pass intelligence information to the MID and ONI, intelligence information he could use to advantage in the bureaucratic battles that were waged among the components of U.S. intelligence.[202]

The unofficial mission of the BSC consisted of numerous covert activities designed for the collection of intelligence and special operations intended to influence the U.S. to enter the war. These activities included the organization of pro-interventionist movements in the U.S., "the direction of subversive propaganda from American sources to Europe and the Far East," and the targeting of prominent isolationists and isolationist organizations using psychological operations.[203] While these activities and the liaison with Hoover may have had some indirect influence on the attitude of the Navy Department toward cooperation with the British, the BSC's assistance in the area of counterintelligence was significant and probably served to positively dispose members of the naval establishment familiar with them toward a closer relationship with the UK. Early in the war, it was a common belief that the Nazi's victories were largely the result of Fifth Column activities. For example, Bradley Smith cites the fact that in all of 1939 there were only 1,600 reports of sabotage submitted to the FBI yet, on a single day after the fall of France in May 1940, there were 2,400 reports made.[204] These beliefs were reinforced, in the minds of senior U.S. leaders, by reports from overseas, which stated without equivocation that the German sweep through Europe was more the result of German propaganda, sabotage, and covert operations than any marked superiority of the German military and its tactics.[205]

After the defeat of France, ONI was even more eager to coordinate with BSC on security matters. The BSC actively sought opportunities to cultivate ONI's

---

[200] BSC, *Secret History,* xxx-xxxi.

[201] BSC, *Secret History,* 241-243.

[202] BSC, *Secret History,* 3-5.

[203] Aldrich, 99-100; BSC, *Secret History,* xxxi-xxxii.

[204] Smith, *Ultra-Magic Deals,* 9-10.

[205] Alan Goodrich Kirk, CAPT, USN, Letter to Rear Admiral Walter S. Anderson, USN, Director of Naval Intelligence, 14 May 1940, *Kirk Papers.*

good will and encouraged greater cooperation to deconflict the efforts of both organizations. For example, the British had run agents on neutral and American shipping to report on subversive activity and smuggling and to spread propaganda. In the Fall of 1941, the agents on the American ships were turned over to ONI's control and a cooperative agreement was reached to share intelligence from these sources and the agents on the neutral ships, which the British still controlled.[206]

The Donovan Visit—15 July 1940–4 August 1940

Bath and others have stated that Colonel William "Wild Bill" Donovan's visit to London in the summer of 1940 was the turning point in the relationship between the U.S. and the UK, a contention the historical evidence confirms.[207] Donovan's mission was to act as an impartial observer to assess England's chances of surviving the war following the fall of France. His positive endorsement of the British and his sanguine assessment of their prospects allowed Roosevelt and other senior officials to overcome their fears of Great Britain's imminent downfall, fears which had been fanned by the negative evaluations of the British situation they were receiving from the U.S. Ambassador to Great Britain, Joseph P. Kennedy, and the naval attaché there, CAPT Kirk.[208]

Why was Donovan chosen to undertake this mission and what was the role of the British in the decision to send him? First, while not a close associate of Roosevelt, Donovan was known by him and the successful World War I hero and Wall Street lawyer was a close personal friend of Secretary of the Navy Knox.[209] William Stephenson was also a friend of Donovan's and, as the head of the BSC, it was his job to counteract the negative assessments of England's chances in the

---

[206] BSC, *Secret History*, 161-165. The BSC also shared intelligence with ONI gained by one of their most sensitive sources, the agent known as "Cynthia," who had deep penetration of the Italian embassy. They also extensively shared information obtained by their Consular Security Officers in Latin American ports with ONI, the Coast Guard, and the FBI. For additional information see BSC, *Secret History*, 214-215, 244-249.

[207] Bath, 27-28; MacLachlan, 225-226; Smith, *Ultra-Magic Deals*, 14-16; Dorwart, *Conflict of Duty*, 144; Corey Ford, *Donovan of OSS* (Boston, MA: Little, Brown, and Company, 1970), 91-94. Donovan would go on to become the head of America's first, official central intelligence organization, the Coordinator of Information office, and would also lead its more famous successor organization, the Office of Strategic Services (OSS).

[208] Beesly, *Very Special Admiral*, 175; Ford, 89.

[209] "Transcript of Press Conference with the Secretary of the Navy, The Honorable Frank Knox," 20 September 1940, *Knox Papers*. Knox had just completed a two-week inspection tour of the U.S. Fleet and told reporters he had brought his personal friend, Colonel William Donovan, with him on the tour.

war that were emanating from the U.S. Embassy in London. Donovan, because of his connections and his pro-British stance, became Stephenson's instrument for doing this.[210] Although both Secretary of War Stimson and Knox did not think the Embassy was providing an accurate assessment of England's chances, they could make no official overtures to the British because of the domestic political climate. During a meeting attended by Knox, Stimson, Donovan, and Stephenson, at which the destroyer-for-bases deal being discussed, Stephenson saw that the main dilemma facing the decisionmakers in the U.S. government was whether England would survive the summer. They required proof "that American material assistance would be, not improvident charity, but a sound investment."[211] To overcome the dilemma, Stephenson suggested sending Donovan on an independent fact-finding mission to Great Britain. Not only was Donovan respected by the President, but as former political opponent of Roosevelt, a Republican, a Catholic, and a Southerner, he was not part of Roosevelt's constituency and his conclusions would be seen as completely independent.[212] Knox presented the idea to the President, who approved the mission. Although he officially traveled as "a personal representative of the Secretary of the Navy," the key decisionmakers on both sides of the Atlantic knew he was traveling at the behest of the President and were well aware of how critical his assessment would be for the relationship between the two countries.[213]

On the day of Donovan's departure, Stephenson cabled the Central Security Service (CSS) headquarters to inform them that Donovan was arriving by steamer and that his evaluation of British prospects would be the key to unlocking the destroyer-for-bases deal and fostering closer cooperation with the Americans.[214] The British at this stage knew far more about the trip than Ambassador Kennedy, who was not informed that Donovan was coming or what the purpose of his trip would be.[215] CAPT Kirk and his staff, however, were aware, given Donovan's official status, and they made many of his arrangements.[216] Kirk and Donovan also had a personal relationship and, while Kirk was concerned that the British

---

[210] Ford, 90; BSC, *Secret History*, 9.

[211] BSC, *Secret History*, 9.

[212] Leutze, *Bargaining for Supremacy*, 97-103; Beesly, *Very Special Admiral*, 176; BSC, *Secret History*, 9; MacLachlan, 225-225.

[213] N. R. Hitchcock, CDR, USN, Assistant Naval Attaché for Air, Memorandum to Air Commodore Boyle, Air Ministry, n.d., *Kirk Papers*. Given its place in the collection and the topic, this memo was probably written between 22-24 July 1940.

[214] BSC, *Secret History*, 9-10.

[215] James Leutze, *The London Journal of General Raymond E. Lee, 1940-1941* (Boston, MA: Little, Brown, and Company, 1971), 19. Cited hereafter as Leutze, *London Journal*.

would merely show Donovan "the best side of the picture," he was confident Donovan would produce a realistic assessment of their situation.[217] Kirk was correct, and while the British did put their best foot forward, they also gave him virtually unrestricted access their military facilities, intelligence organizations, factories, and people from all classes of society so he could accurately assess the British will to fight. He was granted audiences with King George VI, Prime Minister Churchill, various government ministers, industrialists, and labor leaders. Donovan was taken to see Britain's coastal defenses, radar installations, fighter-interceptor bases, and was given full briefings by DNI Godfrey, head of the CSS, Sir Stewart Menzies, and others on a range of intelligence matters to include the functioning of the SIS, British propaganda and SOE activities, and their highly successful counterintelligence activities.[218]

Donovan returned to America on 8 August 1940 and reported to Roosevelt, Stimson, and Knox that the British were well worth the investment in American resources as they had the will to survive. His endorsement is credited with giving Roosevelt the confidence to proceed with the destroyer-for-bases deal and his advocacy for closer intelligence sharing has been seen as a factor in Roosevelt's decision in September 1940 to release U.S. diplomatic and consular reports to the British Ambassador.[219] In addition to aiding the British war effort by encouraging U.S. decisionmakers to bend the rules regarding U.S. neutrality laws, Donovan, upon his return, also co-wrote a series of highly popular articles on the threat from German Fifth Column movements with information he was provided by the SIS. This effort promoted the BSC's covert anti-isolationist propaganda objectives.[220] Donovan would later play an even greater role in the exchange of intelligence between the two countries as the Coordinator for Information and head of the Office of Strategic Services, but this early visit was instrumental in creating conditions that would lead to unprecedented technical and intelligence exchanges

---

[216] Alan Goodrich Kirk, CAPT, USN, Letter to William Donovan, COL, USA (Ret.), 22 July 1940, *Kirk Papers*.

[217] Alan Goodrich Kirk, CAPT, USN, Letter to Rear Admiral Walter S. Anderson, USN, Director of Naval Intelligence, 27 July 1940, *Kirk Papers*, 1-2; Dorwart, *Conflict of Duty*, 143.

[218] Ford, 91; Aldrich, 97; Dorwart, *Conflict of Duty*, 144; BSC, *Secret History*, 10.

[219] Ford, 94; Smith, *Ultra-Magic Deals*, 38. Hinsley also notes that relations between the NID and the U.S. naval attaché office became much closer after Donovan's visit, but there were a number of other factors that aided in creating a closer relationship between the two organizations between August and October of 1940. For additional information see Hinsley, British Intel vol. 1, 312.

[220] BSC, *Secret History*, 5-6; U.S. War Department, History Project, Strategic Services Unit, *War Report of the OSS* (Office of Strategic Services) (New York: Walker and Company, 1976), 11-12. Cited hereafter as *OSS War Report*.

between the two countries, exchanges that were orchestrated by the British to tie the two countries closer together, even though the threat of war was still many months away for the United States.[221]

Special Missions—1940

Numerous individuals in England shared Godfrey's view that the best way to gain the cooperation of the Americans was to make them indebted to the British by providing them information gratis. Two of the most influential individuals were Archibald Vivian (A.V.) Hill and Henry Tizard, two of Great Britain's top scientists. Hill had been sent to America on a secret mission in March 1940 to assess U.S. scientific and technological prowess and production capabilities. By April, Hill was convinced that most Americans were pro-British, despite the prevalence of isolationist sentiments, and that the Americans were not nearly so technologically backward as the British had always assumed.[222] Hill believed it in the best interests of Britain to share technical secrets with America, not just to secure American good will, but also to tap into and guide the tremendous productive capacity of the U.S. to meet England's wartime needs. To implement these ideas, Hill called upon the British Ambassador to the U.S., Lord Lothian, recommending that he contact the Foreign Office to suggest a technical exchange mission to America, with the principal goal of providing the U.S. with British radar technology.[223]

---

[221] Donovan would undertake a second fact-finding mission for the President from December 1940 to March 1941. In addition to visiting England, Donovan traveled extensively through the Mediterranean and the Balkans, assessing the situation in those areas. He became increasingly close to some of the main figures in British intelligence, particularly DNI Godfrey, who advised the commander of British forces in the Mediterranean to show Donovan whatever he wanted to see since, given Donovan's access and pro-British sympathies, Godfrey felt the British could "achieve infinitely more through Donovan than through any other individual." See Ford, 99. Donovan's experience with British intelligence would also persuade him that the U.S. also needed a central intelligence organization, an idea he began to advocate with increasing success upon his return to America in March 1941. Donovan was designated Coordinator for Information in July 1941 and head of the OSS in June 1942. For additional information see Jay Jakub, *Spies and Saboteurs: Anglo-American Collaboration and Rivalry in Human Intelligence Collection and Special Operation,1940-45* (New York: St. Martin's Press, Inc., 1999), 1; Aldrich, 98-99; Ford, 107-108; OSS War Report, 6-7; BSC, *Secret History*, 13-15.

[222] Zimmerman, 50, 54.

[223] Zimmerman, 53-56. Lord Lothian (Philip Kerr) was a supporter of a U.S.-UK alliance and he had many influential friends among the American elite, especially Roosevelt's close friend, Felix Frankfurter. For additional information see Zimmerman, 53-54.

Lothian passed Hill's proposal to the Foreign Office, where it was intensely debated. Tizard, who worked for the Air Ministry and was essentially the creator of Great Britain's air defense early warning network, was adamant about the need to engage in this exchange. While many, including Churchill, were opposed to an exchange, particularly one offered with no expectation of reciprocation, Tizard was aided in his fight by other high-ranking individuals, such as First Sea Lord, Sir Dudley Pound, who persuasively argued that concerns about U.S. security were overblown. By late June, Churchill gave his permission for the mission to go forward, most likely in response to the worsening military situation.[224] Tizard was placed in charge of the mission and given the go-ahead to begin planning for the exchanges.[225] On 8 July 1940, Lord Lothian presented an aide-memoire to the State Department, requesting an immediate and general exchange of technical information between the two governments. Significantly, the proposal stated that

> [i]t is not the wish of His Majesty's Government to make this proposal the subject of a bargain of any description. Rather do they wish, in order to show their readiness for the fullest cooperation, to be perfectly open with you and to give you full details of any equipment or devices in which you are interested without in any way pressing you before hand to give specific undertakings on your side, although, of course, they would hope you could reciprocate.[226]

Further, Lothian made it clear that the British were offering to provide the Americans with their most important technical secret, radar, as the proposal stated the British were willing to give the Americans techniques used to detect and target enemy aircraft.[227] Here the British made it clear that there would be no quid pro quo in this exchange, that the information they would provide would be gratis and that it would be as full and complete as the Americans desired.

Both the Navy and the War Departments accepted the British proposal. The official U.S. acceptance was sent to the British on 29 July 1940, designating the

---

[224] Zimmerman, 20-24, 62-64, 71, 117.

[225] Leutze, "Technology and Bargaining," 57-58.

[226] Department of State, "The British Ambassador (Lothian) to President Roosevelt—Aide Memoire," 8 July 1940, in *Foreign Relations of the United States 1940 3* (Washington, DC: GPO, 1958): 78. Cited hereafter as "Aide Memoire, 8 July 1940," *FRUS 1940* vol. 3.

[227] "Aide Memoire, 8 July 1940," *FRUS 1940* vol. 3, 78.

U.S. DNI, RADM Anderson, as the Navy's lead representative for the technical exchanges.[228] Demonstrating the distrust and technical chauvinism characteristic of many in the U.S. Navy at this time, the Navy's internal assessment was that Tizard's Mission was most likely a ploy on the part of the British to gain access to U.S. industry and Rear Admiral H. G. Bowen, the Director of the Navy Research Lab (NRL), believed the Navy would get little from the exchange, given American technological superiority.[229] The Navy's assessment would be proved wrong.

Tizard left the UK on 14 August 1940 and, while his team was heavily slanted toward experts in radar, his group was given permission to provide the Americans with information on 21 different technologies, to include anti-aircraft guns, armor plating, self-sealing fuel tanks, and gyroscopic gunsights—all of which had been tested in the field of battle. Tizard's mission was classified as Top Secret, since any word of the exchange would likely inflame U.S. isolationists.[230]

The Tizard Mission began on 29 August 1940. The first meetings concerned asdic, sonar, and anti-submarine warfare. While reticent at first, by the afternoon of the first day the U.S. team had warmed to their British visitors and were quite excited about exploring the possibility of combining the two countries' research efforts on sonar and asdic, as both sides had taken different, but complementary, approaches to the submarine detection problem. That same day, the British also described advances they had made in radar, which completely impressed the Americans.[231] However, U.S. distrust of the British was

---

[228] Department of State, "The Acting Secretary of State to the British Ambassador (Lothian)," 29 July 1940, *FRUS 1940* vol. 3, 79; Leutze, "Technology and Bargaining," 57; Zimmerman, 76-77. Amazingly, as David Zimmerman relates in his comprehensive study of the Tizard Mission, *Top Secret Exchange*, Churchill almost scuttled the Tizard Mission before the U.S. was able to officially accept it. Demonstrating all of the British attitudes that inhibited cooperation between the two countries in the period before the U.S. entered the war, Churchill on 17 July 1940 wrote to his Chiefs of Staff liaison, GEN Ismay, querying why his advisors were so quick to toss away Britain's precious secrets to the U.S. when the U.S. was so loath to give anything back. He also noted the superiority of British technology to anything America possessed and demonstrated substantial resentment that the U.S. was still far away from entering the war. Churchill also expressed grave reservations over U.S. security, commenting that anything they gave the Americans would soon find its way to Germany. Churchill's correspondence to Ismay stands in marked contrast to his more famous letters to Roosevelt, in which he displays, for obvious reasons, none of the distrust and resentment of America that is evident from this incident. Progress on Roosevelt's destroyers-for-bases deal allowed Churchill to overcome his pique and give final approval to the mission. For additional information see Zimmerman, 82.

[229] Zimmerman, 46-47.

[230] Zimmerman, 94-95, 98

[231] Zimmerman, 102-105.

still a powerful influence. While Zimmerman has written that the Navy removed many of their restrictions concerning the sharing of U.S. technology by 4 September 1940, a 16 September 1940 memorandum from DNI Anderson to the head of the U.S. National Defense Research Council (NDRC), Dr. Vannevar Bush, made it clear that the NDRC was not to discuss any Navy technologies with the British without Navy Department personnel present, that the NDRC must not discuss anything on the Navy's list of topics prohibited for discussion, and that there must be nothing discussed about capabilities in development.[232] Bush replied two days later, stating the NDRC would respect the Navy's policy but was hopeful it would change "since all of the work of the Committee has to do with development, and since "I [Bush] believe that the discussions on such matters are likely to be of particular benefit."[233]

By the end of September, the rest of Tizard's team had arrived in the U.S. and sometime around 27 September, Tizard presented his American hosts with a "resonant cavity magnetron," the key component for constructing a microwave radar, a piece of technology the U.S. was still months, if not years, away from developing independently.[234] Both Zimmerman and Leutze contend that this magnanimous gift and the free and open exchange of other information the British provided during the month proceeding its delivery, completely changed the attitude of the Navy and War Departments with regard to sharing of technical information.[235] The archival data confirm this assessment. On 28 September 1940, Secretary of the Navy Frank Knox issued a letter concerning the Tizard Mission to all the bureaus of the Navy staff. In that letter, he cancelled all restrictions on the provision of technical information to Great Britain with the exception of the Norden bombsight and the antenna mine, which were to remain secret. Knox's reasoning, much like Kirk's, was that the British should be given "drawings, specifications, performance data and any other detailed information" concerning U.S. technologies because "advantages...will accrue to [the United States] in the matter of procurement and combat tests."[236] By October, even the pessimistic RADM Bowen was won over by the liberality of the

---

[232] Walter S. Anderson, RADM, USN, Director of Naval Intelligence, Letter to Dr. Vannevar Bush, 16 September 1940, *DNI Correspondence*; Zimmerman, 106. The NDRC was formed by Roosevelt earlier in 1940. A civilian organization formed at Roosevelt's direction, its charter was similar to today's Defense Advanced Research Projects Agency (DARPA). Although the NDRC was not supposed to duplicate research being done by the military service labs, there was distrust between the labs and the NDRC, as indicated by Anderson's concerns that members of the NDRC were meeting independently with members of the Tizard mission.

[233] Dr. Vannevar Bush, Letter to Rear Admiral Walter S. Anderson, USN, Director of Naval Intelligence, 18 September 1940, *DNI Correspondence*.

[234] Leutze, "Technology and Bargaining," 58.

[235] Leutze, "Technology and Bargaining," 5859; Zimmerman, 124-129.

[236] Frank Knox, Secretary of the Navy, Letter to All Navy Bureaus and Directors, 28 September 1940, *DNI Correspondence*, 1-2.

exchanges and emphasized to Knox that the U.S. was getting the better part of the deal with the British.[237]

While details concerning the limits and mechanisms of exchange would remain issues, the Tizard Mission and the concurrent Standardization of Arms Talks broke the logjam concerning the stationing of British observers on U.S. ships.[238] Starting in late July 1940, the British had begun allowing U.S. naval observers access to their ships and facilities, without requesting a reciprocal agreement from the U.S. Navy.[239] By October, the decision was made to allow British observers with the U.S. Fleet. The Commander of the U.S. Fleet was notified of the Tizard Mission and told that "British observers...should be afforded a reasonable opportunity to observe the operation and application of instruments, devices and systems, and that they may be acquainted with Operational experience with regard to such matters."[240] This policy was significantly different from that used during CAPT Ellis' visit during the boom defense-arresting gear exchange 16 months previously. Information related to codes and ciphers was still off limits but, otherwise, commanders were given "a large degree of discretionary latitude" in the release of information to the British observers.[241]

---

[237] Zimmerman, 121-123.

[238] Many of the limitations on fuller technical information exchange after this stage would be due to licensing and manufacturing agreements, which legally restricted some of the information that could be provided on both the U.S. and British sides. Problems with the mechanics of exchange became apparent as the diversity and breadth of the exchanges grew. Given that the U.S. had three main organizations engaged in the exchange, it was only natural that there would be seams between the policies for exchange developed by the Navy and War Departments and the NDRC. For additional information see Dr. Vannevar Bush, Letter to Admiral Harold Stark, USN, Chief of Naval Operations, 30 September 1940, *DNI Correspondence*, 1-2; Walter S. Anderson, RADM, USN, Director of Naval Intelligence, Letter to Chief of Bureau of Aeronautics, 5 October 1940, *DNI Correspondence*, 1-2; Walter S. Anderson, RADM, USN, Director of Naval Intelligence, Letter to Bureau Chiefs and Division Directors, 14 November 1940, *DNI Correspondence*, 1-2.

[239] Alan Goodrich Kirk, CAPT, USN. Letter to Rear Admiral Walter S. Anderson, USN, Director of Naval Intelligence, 27 July 1940, *Kirk Papers*, 1-2. The British had actually agreed to accept U.S. naval observers on a non-reciprocal basis at the start of the war in September 1939. It would be July 1940, however, before the British allowed the first observers to come over, a source of great frustration to Kirk. Eventually, the observer force in the UK would number in the hundreds and would be a critical source of intelligence for ONI. For additional information see Alan Goodrich Kirk, CAPT, USN, Letter to Rear Admiral Walter S. Anderson, USN, Director of Naval Intelligence, 4 November 1939, *Kirk Papers*; Alan Goodrich Kirk, CAPT, USN, Letter to Rear Admiral Walter S. Anderson, USN, Director of Naval Intelligence, 29 February 1940, *Kirk Papers*, 1; Alan Goodrich Kirk, CAPT, USN, Letter to Rear Admiral Walter S. Anderson, USN, Director of Naval Intelligence, 10 June 1940, *Kirk Papers*, 1-2; Leutze, *Bargaining for Supremacy*, 59; Leutze, "Technology and Bargaining," 53.

[240] Harold Stark, ADM, Chief of Naval Operations, Letter to Commander in Chief, United States Fleet, 3 October 1940, *DNI Correspondence*, 1-2. Cited hereafter as "Stark Letter," 3 October 1940, *DNI Correspondence*

[241] "Stark Letter," 3 October 1940, *DNI Correspondence*, 2.

Since the Tizard Mission had only a temporary mandate, the two U.S. military departments and the NDRC were extremely interested in setting up permanent technical exchange missions, as the benefits of the cooperative endeavor were so manifest. In October 1940, Knox and Secretary of War Stimson formalized their agreement on the exchange of technical secrets with the British and, in November, the Navy notified Professor Cockroft, Tizard's successor, that the Navy desired to continue with technical exchanges on a permanent basis.[242] In January 1941, the British made non-reciprocal exchange of information with the Americans a standing policy and by April 1941, the Navy's desires concerning a permanent exchange mechanism had become a reality when a U.S. technical exchange mission, under Dr. James Conant of the NDRC, was established in London and a similar British mission, under Sir Charles Darwin, was established in Washington DC.[243] In large measure, this mission burst the shackles of mistrust and bargaining that had inhibited the exchange of information between the two countries. The Tizard Mission was designed to exchange technical secrets, but a significant amount of general intelligence was also shared during the course of this undertaking.[244]

Zimmerman's final assessment of the Tizard Mission was that it did much to alleviate the deep mistrust the two countries had for one another and "played a critical part in building the special relationship that characterized the Western Alliance."[245] The archival evidence and the research done by James Leutze bear out Zimmerman's contention, as the period from August to October 1940 demonstrated a marked change in the attitudes of the Navy Department concerning information exchange with their British counterparts. As evidenced by Knox's letter and RADM Bowen's reactions, the British openness had a positive effect on the Americans and vindicated the policies that Godfrey, Tizard, Hill, and Pound had advocated so strenuously. The Tizard Mission was just one of a number of British attempts to tie America more closely to its war effort. Other efforts, such as the Standardization of Arms Talks, would set the stage for the move toward alliance in 1941.

---

[242] Leutze, "Technology and Bargaining," 59; Walter S. Anderson, RADM, USN, Director of Naval Intelligence, Letter to Professor Cockroft, 20 November 1940, *DNI Correspondence*, 1.

[243] Zimmerman, 182; Leutze, "Technology and Bargaining," 60.

[244] Although the Tizard Mission primarily focused on exchanging scientific secrets, it also addressed the exchange of information about specific capabilities that each of the countries possessed, capabilities developed to address the threats identified by their intelligence organizations. Moreover, the British briefings on their capabilities would follow a pattern whereby a scientist would brief the technology and an operator would brief on the employment of the system in actual combat, sometimes accompanied by a film of the system being used against the Germans. These briefings had a very powerful effect on the Americans, as they contained valuable intelligence in addition to useful technical information. For additional information see Zimmerman, 120-121.

[245] Zimmerman, 6.

Standardization of Arms Talks—15-31 August 1940

The Standardization of Arms Talks was the cover name for secret staff talks held between the military services of the U.S. and the UK in the late summer of 1940. As with the Tizard Mission, these talks came as the result of a suggestion made to Roosevelt by the British Ambassador, Lord Lothian. In a meeting with the President and the Secretary of State on 11 June 1940, Lothian informed Roosevelt "that he [Lothian] had received from Mr. Churchill...a suggestion that there might be staff conferences between the naval people of our two governments in regard to fleet movements both in the Atlantic and the Pacific."[246] Interestingly, after Roosevelt had agreed to these talks, there was some discussion on the British side as to whether these informal staff talks should be combined with Tizard's technical exchange mission, which would occur almost concurrently. The British Foreign Office persuasively argued against taking this tack, noting that engagement with the Americans on as many levels as possible was needed to obtain U.S. cooperation.[247]

Why did U.S. policymakers accede to this particular request, especially when they had been so sensitive to any tilt toward England during this election year? While Donovan's reports on the British ability to prevail in the war were certainly influential in alleviating U.S. fears that the secrets they provided Britain would not rapidly fall into enemy hands, the U.S. delegation had in fact left for England on 12 July 1940, which was before Donovan arrived in London, making it doubtful that Donovan's reports on the situation in England played a role in the decision to send the delegation, as Dorwart suggests.[248] The fall of France, however, had a major impact on the psyche of American policymakers and the American people. Congress responded to the fears generated by France's downfall by

---

[246] Department of State, "Memorandum of Conversation, by the Secretary of State," 11 June 1940, in *FRUS 1940* vol. 3, 36. There is some confusion in the literature as to when this offer was made, although the archival data clearly show an official offer was made on 11 June 1940 and this information is consistent with that found in the Commander Naval Forces, Europe Administrative History. James Leutze contends the offer was made in May 1940, which may have happened, although it is unclear why this second offer would have been necessary if Roosevelt had accepted then, or why it would be proffered again if Roosevelt had rejected it just weeks before. Ralph Erskine states the offer was made to COL William Donovan during his visit to London in July, although this is unlikely as preparations for the visit of the U.S. delegation were already being made by the time Donovan arrived in England. For additional information see *COMNAVEU Admin History*, 1; Leutze, "Technology and Bargaining," 57; Ralph Erskine, "Churchill and the Start of the Ultra-Magic Deals," *International Journal of Intelligence and Counterintelligence 10*, no. 1 (Spring 1997): 58.

[247] Zimmerman, 82-83.

[248] Morison, *The Battle of the Atlantic*, 40-41; Dorwart, 143.

appropriating large increases to the defense budget.[249] This was not enough, however. The Army and Navy, in their 1 July 1940 assessment "Are We Ready-II," determined that the "the emergency now faced is one of worldwide dimensions which menaces every foreign policy of the United States" and concluded that, despite the influx of additional funds, the military was unprepared for war.[250] Given this fact, Roosevelt and his advisors determined that it was best to establish the groundwork for cooperation prior to the U.S. entry into the war, as attempting to do so would alleviate many of the problems the U.S. experienced in World War I when trying to integrate their forces with the allied powers.[251] This position was reinforced by the attaché reports they were receiving from Kirk, who articulately relayed his assessment that Dutch and Belgian refusals to hold staff talks with the British and French prior to the German invasion of those countries was a major factor in their defeat and the eventual rout of the allied powers in France.[252]

The fall of France also changed the direction of U.S. strategic thinking, shifting the focus from the Far East to the European theater. Although it is unknown how much impact his report may have had, Kirk wrote a persuasive assessment of the strategic situation in late June 1940 that recommended an Atlantic-first strategy months before Stark's Plan Dog memo outlined the new U.S. strategic policy. Kirk noted that the British firmly believed the U.S. would enter on their side at some stage and they were committed to holding the islands as a base from which the U.S. could project offensive power. Looking at the global situation, Kirk assessed the British Isles as the true center of gravity for the allies in the war, reasoning that everything on the periphery of the British Empire could be sacrificed but if the Home Islands were lost, it was unlikely the Axis would be defeated.[253] Kirk was certainly not alone in seeing how the fall of France had altered the strategic landscape for the U.S., but his opinion did reach high-level policymakers in the U.S. government, who respected his judgment. Though they had rejected his advice previously due to domestic political constraints, after the fall of France U.S. policymakers felt they had far more latitude to explore a cooperative partnership with Britain than they had available to them at the start of the war.

---

[249] Reynolds, 109..

[250] Chairman, General Board, "Are We Ready—II," 1 July 1940, *Strategic Planning.*

[251] Morison, *The Battle of the Atlantic*, 39.

[252] Ian Goodrich Kirk, CAPT, USN, Letter to Rear Admiral Walter S. Anderson, USN, Director of Naval Intelligence, 14 May 1940, *Kirk Papers*; Alan Goodrich Kirk, CAPT, USN, Letter to Rear Admiral Walter S. Anderson, USN, Director of Naval Intelligence, 1 June 1940, *Kirk Papers*, 1-2. In this same report, Kirk also noted the improvement in intelligence cooperation with the British, stating how the embassy was being routinely provided the daily intelligence summary given to the British War Cabinet by June 1940.

[253] Alan Goodrich Kirk, CAPT, USN, Letter to Rear Admiral Walter S. Anderson, USN, Director of Naval Intelligence, 24 June 1940, *Kirk Papers*, 1.

The U.S. delegation to the Standardization of Arms talks left the U.S. on 12 July 1940 and arrived in England on 15 August. The senior naval representative was Rear Admiral Robert Ghormley, a former Director of War Plans. The delegation was given its orders by the President, who designated Ghormley as the naval attaché, although this designation was changed to Special Naval Observer (SPECNO) just before his arrival, to highlight the distinction between his role and that of Kirk.[254] Ghormley was accompanied by Brigadier General G. V. Strong, from the U.S. Army, and Major General C. Emmons, from the U.S. Army Air Corps. In their first meeting with the British, held on 20 August 1940, Ghormley made it clear that these were not considered formal talks by the U.S. government and that he and the two generals were there as representatives from their individual Services, not as part of a Joint delegation. The British responded that they understood this and told the U.S. delegation that, from 21 to 28 August, they would be taken to the headquarters of the three services to see various operational units. The Americans were encouraged to ask questions and were told to request additions to the agenda if there were organizations or capabilities they would like to see that were not included on the proposed schedule.[255] As with the Donovan visit, which had concluded earlier in the month, and the Tizard Mission, which would begin in the U.S. just days later, the British policy was to hold little back from the Americans, hopeful that their openness would produce the cooperation they sought.

On 23 August, Ghormley forwarded a report to the CNO from the British concerning the conduct of the war to that point. Ghormley did not comment on the report, but it was exceptionally honest about British objectives throughout the first year of the war and the miscalculations that had led to defeat. In this brief, the British reiterated the point that Kirk had made: that the failure to successfully conclude staff talks with the Dutch and the Belgians before the Germans attacked was a key element in their defeat on the Continent. The British also made sure the U.S. knew that they had subordinated the British Expeditionary Force (B.E.F.) to

---

[254] Albion, 550; *COMNAVEU Administrative History*, 1-2. Roosevelt appears to have believed that Ghormley, as the senior naval officer in England, would need to have the status of the naval attaché position. Although Kirk made no official comment about how this action would cause him to lose face with the British, he mentioned it to Donovan, who arranged to have Stark write a letter to the President which outlined the situation and recommended changing Ghormley's designation to SPECNO. Roosevelt concurred with the decision. Recalling the situation years later, Kirk stated that this in no way affected his working relationship with Ghormley, who was an old friend. For additional information see Harold Stark, ADM, Chief of Naval Operations, Memorandum to the President of the United States, 8 August 1940; Kirk Papers, 1; Alan Goodrich Kirk, CAPT, USN, Letter to William Donovan, 14 August 1940, *Kirk Papers*, 1; *Kirk Reminiscences*, 166-167.

[255] Standardization of Arms Committee, "1st Meeting of the Anglo-American Standardization of Arms Committee," 20 August 1940, *Strategic Planning*, 1-3; 5. Kirk and the U.S. Army Attaché COL Raymond E. Lee, were also present at all of the Standardization of Arms Committee meetings.

the French, a point which would not be lost on the Americans since they were very concerned about British attempts to dominate any command and control relationships that might be established whenever the military forces of the two countries would operate together. Additionally, the report outlined Great Britain's situation and provided general intelligence concerning shipping losses and effective tactics against German bombers.[256]

After the tours were concluded, the Committee reconvened on 29 August and the British laid out their view of the strategic situation in a frank and wide-ranging brief. The British identified their two strategic priorities as defense of the Home Islands and Egypt, noting that there was little they could do to improve their situation in the Far East. They were sanguine about their prospects, believing that the war would be won by the country that could make the most effective use of superior resources and noting that their control of the seas gave them access to all the world's resources and American productive capacity while the Germans could only draw on the resources of Europe. During the presentation, the British candidly answered questions about their procurement programs, scope of U.S. assistance desired, and the effectiveness of their own blockade efforts.[257] Once again, the candor of the British, along with their optimism and confidence, even in the face of the London Blitz, which was then beginning, appeared to have a positive effect on the U.S. delegation.

From the perspective of intelligence cooperation between the two countries, the subsequent meeting held on 31 August was a watershed event. This meeting began with the British outlining their general strategy for winning the war and reiterating the position they had taken during the 1939 talks between the CNO and CDR Hampton: that they would need to rely heavily on the U.S. in the Far East if Japan initiated hostilities there. Ghormley asked the British a number of tough questions concerning their expectations of the U.S., all of which the British answered with candor.[258] BGEN Strong made an offer that would eventually help to forge the SIGINT relationship between the two countries. He told the British that

---

[256] Robert Ghormley, RADM, USN, Memorandum to Admiral Harold Stark, USN, Chief of Naval Operations, 23 August 1940, *Strategic Planning*, 1-11. Ghormley forwarded the report on the conduct of the war, which the British had prepared on 16 August 1940, to Stark as an enclosure to this memo.

[257] Standardization of Arms Committee, "Minutes of the Anglo-American Standardization of Arms Committee," 29 August 1940, *Strategic Planning*, 1-11.

[258] Standardization of Arms Committee, "Minutes of the Anglo-American Standardization of Arms Committee," 31 August 1940, *Strategic Planning*, 1-12. Cited hereafter as *SOA Committee Minutes*, 31 August 1940.

it had recently been agreed in principle between the British and United States Governments that a periodical [sic] exchange of information would be desirable. He...thought the time had now come when this exchange of information should be placed on a regular basis. He outlined certain methods by which sources of information at the disposal of the United States might be placed at the disposal of the British Government.[259]

Although Strong's full comments have been merely summarized here, both the literature and the archival evidence are in agreement that Strong was discussing SIGINT sources and methods.[260] Although the U.S. and the UK had exchanged information on lower-level SIGINT capabilities, such as HF/DF, what Strong was proposing was the sharing of the higher-level COMINT capabilities both states possessed as well as the "take" from those sources.[261] Given the sensitivities involved with discussing SIGINT, an information exchange agreement on this topic would take months to conclude, but it would mark the start of a relationship that would bring tremendous benefits for both countries in the long term.

In the short term, the Standardization of Arms Talks did not produce tangible results for the British. They were pleased that the destroyer-for-bases deal had been concluded successfully, but the British had hoped for some more substantive commitments from the Americans as a result of these talks.[262] Still, the talks represented a significant step forward as they allowed the U.S. to see the depth of British strategic thought and they renewed U.S. confidence that the British would survive the war. Following the conclusion of the talks, the British gave permission for a large influx of U.S. observers and, even more significantly,

---

[259] *SOA Committee Minutes*, 31 August 1940, 11.

[260] Hinsley, *British Intel* vol. 1, 312; Leutze, "Technology and Bargaining," 58; Smith, *Ultra-Magic Deals*, 74; Erskine, 58. RADM Ghormley was taken aback by Strong's offer, writing to Stark that he didn't let the British Chiefs of Staff see his surprise "as I did not want them to know or suspect that Strong was taking the initiative in something which I would not have done." Robert Ghormley, RADM, USN, Letter to Admiral Harold Stark, USN, Chief of Naval Operations, 23 October 1940, *Strategic Planning*, 2.

[261] Hinsley notes that the British were reluctantly providing the Dominions Wire, an all-source (including SIGINT) intelligence product to both Roosevelt, through the British Ambassador, and to the U.S. Ambassador, through the Foreign Office, by August 1940. Roosevelt reciprocated by instructing the State Department to release diplomatic and consular reporting to the British. So, while the U.S. was probably receiving some analyzed information from British SIGINT sources at the time of Strong's offer, the product they were provided was sanitized to remove indications there was SIGINT-derived information in it. For additional information see Hinsley, *British Intel,* vol. 1, 312-313.

[262] Leutze, "Technology and Bargaining," 58.

requested that RADM Ghormley remain in Britain so that he could liaise with the Joint Bailey Committee, a temporary organization that would become the major vehicle for information exchange between the two countries prior to the formal ABC-1 staff talks.[263]

The Joint Bailey Committee

On 15 June 1940, the British had established a Joint Committee under Admiral Sir Sydney Bailey to examine the "matter of implementing Anglo-American naval cooperation in the event the United States entered the war."[264] Following the Standardization of Arms Talks on 31 August 1940, RADM Ghormley met with his counterparts on the Admiralty staff to continue technical discussions on the requirements identified by Bailey's committee. Much to Ghormley's surprise, on 2 September 1940, he was provided a copy of Bailey's report by the First Sea Lord, ADM Pound. Ghormley realized the sensitivity of this document, telling Stark that it "was not written in such form as it would have been had it been the intent of the Committee that this text should at any time have been handed to me" and notified Stark that he would continue unofficial talks with the British, given their openness in discussing a host of operational, technical, and intelligence matters.[265] Ghormley returned to the U.S. in January to prepare for the ABC-1 staff talks, but the process for information exchange established by the Joint Bailey Committee would remain one of the main forums for information sharing well into 1941.

In all, over 400 requests for information from the Committee to the U.S. Navy and over 300 requests for information from the U.S. Navy to the Committee would be processed by the U.S. naval attaché office in London.[266] The topics covered by the Committee were extensive, if not all-inclusive. Requests for information on subjects such as anti-submarine warfare; command, control, and communications; gunnery; damage control; anti-air warfare; amphibious warfare; engineering; operations; tactics; and training were made and honored through the mechanisms established by the Committee.[267] It became one of the main vehicles

---

[263] Beesly, *Very Special Admiral,* 178-179.

[264] *COMNAVEU Administrative History,* 3; Department of the Navy, "Chronological Summary of Events, 15 June 1940-9 October 1940—Admiral Ghormley's Secret Staff Talks," n.d., *Stark Papers.* Cited hereafter as "Chronological Summary of Events," *Stark Papers.*

[265] "Chronological Summary of Events," *Stark Papers*; Robert Ghormley, RADM, USN, Letter to Admiral Harold Stark, USN, Chief of Naval Operations, 18 September 1940, *Strategic Planning,* 1-2.

[266] Packard, 73; Bath, 44; *COMNAVEU Administrative History,* 5.

by which British combat experience was transmitted to the technical bureaus and the operating forces back in America.

Ghormley personally met with the Committee some 14 times between September and October 1940. Although unofficial, these talks became the basis for the ABC-1 staff talks that were to occur after the New Year. Rather than deal with specific technical exchanges, these meetings concentrated on the various areas in which the Bailey report recommended cooperation with America, to prepare for the eventual U.S. entry into the war. As Kirk had done in his reports from earlier in the year, Ghormley related to the CNO how impressed he was with the British willingness to provide information and their determination to see the war through to the end. Although the exchange was going well, he did have some major concerns. What alarmed him most was the possibility the British would cut off the exchange due to a lack of reciprocation. While he had relatively free access to any information he wanted, he had heard reports that the British naval attaché, RADM Pott, had been treated poorly. He wrote to Stark that

---

[267] "Memorandum for Admiral Bailey's Committee No. 1," Subject: H.M.S. Hermes, 12 September 1940; Records of the Naval Operating Forces, U.S. Naval Forces Europe Subject File: From Bailey Committee thru Bolero, Record Group 313; Stack Area 370, Row 30, Compartment 1, Shelf 05, NN3-38-90-3; National Archives Building, College Park Maryland, collection cited hereafter as *Bailey Committee Memos*; "Memorandum for Admiral Bailey's Committee No. 2," Subject: Radio Frequencies, 12 September 1940; *Bailey Committee Memos*; "Memorandum for Admiral Bailey's Committee No. 3," Subject: Royal Navy Publications, 12 September 1940; *Bailey Committee Memos*; "Memorandum for Admiral Bailey's Committee No. 5," Subject: Information on Landing Operations in Norway, 12 September 1940; *Bailey Committee Memos*; "Memorandum for Admiral Bailey's Committee No. 11," Subject: Anti-aircraft Projectiles Containing Wire, 14 September 1940; *Bailey Committee Memos*; "Memorandum for Admiral Bailey's Committee No. 13," Subject: Asdic Pamphlets, 19 September 1940; *Bailey Committee Memos*; "Memorandum for Admiral Bailey's Committee No. 19," Subject: Asdic Attack Teacher Plans, 21 September 1940; *Bailey Committee Memos*; "Memorandum for Admiral Bailey's Committee No. 25," Subject: New Construction, 7 October 1940; *Bailey Committee Memos*; "Memorandum for Admiral Bailey's Committee No. 26," Subject: Dakar Operations, 7 October 1940; *Bailey Committee Memos*.

when he [Pott] comes to O.N.I. he is very restricted in his movements, notes are taken on all his conversations, and information is not freely given to him....Here the Admiralty receives Kirk's representatives with open arms. Some in fact have desks in the Admiralty so that there is no information which is asked for which is not given, and much in addition.[268]

Ghormley was also troubled by the fact that information being sent over by Kirk was being locked in safes at ONI, rather than being sent to the technical bureaus where they were needed. Using language reminiscent of that used by Kirk in the spring, he concluded that "this war laboratory...is bringing forth new lessons every day" and feared the Navy was losing a golden opportunity to improve its readiness for war if the information was not properly disseminated.[269]

The sixth meeting of the Joint Bailey Committee, held on 23 September 1940, specifically concerned intelligence liaison. A number of decisions were made during the course of this meeting. The major achievement was the agreement to establish liaison missions in the intelligence centers of each country once it looked like America was close to entering the war. To support the exchange of information between intelligence facilities, the British informed the U.S. they had developed a special code table for secure communication among intelligence centers and they decided to pre-stage these codes so that they could be rapidly issued to the Americans once the liaison missions were established.[270] Recommendations were also made to continue sharing information on HF/DF stations, with the eventual goal being the evolution of a common organization for exploitation of this source.[271] Although it would be a long time before any of these recommenda-

---

[268] Robert Ghormley, RADM, USN, Memorandum to Admiral Harold Stark, USN, Chief of Naval Operations, 20 September 1940, *Strategic Planning*. Cited hereafter as Ghormley, "Memo to Stark," 20 September 1940. ONI was not the only organization to frustrate RADM Pott, who found the lack of a central intelligence organization, like the British JIC, a major stumbling block in the exchange of information with the Americans. ONI eventually issued guidance, almost 2 months after Ghormley's missive to Stark cited above, to all the Navy's bureaus, instructing them to give Admiral Pott full cooperation on a number of technical matters, to include low-level SIGINT. For additional information see Beesly, *Very Special Admiral*, 180; Walter S. Anderson, RADM, USN, Director of Naval Intelligence, Letter to All Naval Bureau Chiefs and Directors of Divisions, 12 November 1940, *DNI Correspondence*; Robert Ghormley, RADM, USN, Memorandum to Admiral Harold Stark, USN, Chief of Naval Operations, 14 November 1940, *Strategic Planning*.

[269] Ghormley, "Memo to Stark," 20 September 1940, *Strategic Planning*.

[270] "B. C. (JG) Sixth Meeting, United States Naval Co-operation, Minutes of Meeting held on Monday, 23rd September, 1940," 23 September 1940, Subject: British and U.S. Intelligence Liaison, *Strategic Planning*, 1-3. Cited hereafter as "Bailey Committee 6th Meeting Minutes," *Strategic Planning*.

tions would be implemented, the fact that the British and the Americans were willing to consider this closer relationship was a significant change from conditions a year earlier.

The last meeting of the Bailey Committee on 16 October 1940 also concerned intelligence but was specifically focused on "the general interchange of intelligence between the British and United States naval authorities in the Far East."[272] Discussions centered around ways that Far East intelligence cooperation could be enhanced, focusing on the possibility of establishing liaison officers between the Far East commands and establishing a secure method of exchanging intelligence. Recommendations were also made to instruct the U.S. and British naval attachés in Tokyo to liberalize their information exchange and to have ONI and NID exchange any monographs they possessed on Japan and the mandated islands in the Pacific under its control.[273] To support U.S. planning efforts for action against Japan, Ghormley forwarded a complete disposition of all British forces in the Far East as well as the latest British intelligence estimates on the disposition of Dutch forces in the Pacific.[274] While CNO Stark was unimpressed with the "British Far Eastern War Plan [which]...shows much evidence of their usual wishful thinking," he instructed the Commander of the Asiatic Fleet, Admiral T. C. Hart, to develop a framework for cooperation with the British in the Far East and congratulated Ghormley for convincing "the British that there is a Western Pacific in which the United States is interested and in which they also have a great interest."[275]

While Stark still obviously had disdain for the British, he did not let his personal feelings get in the way of his strategic vision. This was the same period during which he completed the Plan Dog Memo, which outlined the framework of the Atlantic-first strategy, centered on cooperation with the British. Stark forwarded a copy of the plan to Ghormley, stating that he could share its existence and contents with the British, but he was not to show it to them in its entirety as

---

[271] "Bailey Committee 6th Meeting Minutes," *Strategic Planning*, 2-3.

[272] "B. C. I. Fourteenth Meeting, United States Naval Co-operation, Minutes of Meeting held on Wednesday, 16th October, 1940," 16 October, *Strategic Planning*, 1. Cited hereafter as "Bailey Committee 14th Meeting Minutes," *Strategic Planning*.

[273] "Bailey Committee 14th Meeting Minutes," *Strategic Planning*, 1-2.

[274] Robert Ghormley, RADM, USN, Memorandum to Admiral Harold Stark, USN, Chief of Naval Operations, 30 October 1940, *Strategic Planning*.

[275] Harold Stark, ADM, USN, Chief of Naval Operations, Letter to Captain T. C. Hart, USN, Commander in Chief, U.S. Asiatic Fleet, 12 November 1940, *Stark Papers*, 1; Harold Stark, ADM, USN, Chief of Naval Operations, Letter to Rear Admiral Robert Ghormley, USN, 16 November 1940, *Stark Papers*. Cited hereafter as "Stark Letter to Ghormley," 16 November 1940, *Stark Papers*.

it was not official U.S. policy. Stark clearly saw that there was a need to formalize all the work Ghormley had done, or the U.S. Navy would be ill-prepared to cooperate with the British when the two countries became allies.[276] Soon after this, with the election now behind the President, the U.S. acceded to the British request, made long ago, for formal staff talks.[277] Stark notified Ghormley, telling him to let the British know these would be frank and honest discussions between equals.[278] Ghormley and Kirk, through the Standardization of Arms Talks and the Bailey Committee, had laid the groundwork for alliance and the British efforts to entice the U.S. into cooperation were now beginning to bear fruit. Although these new staff talks would also remain secret, Ghormley and Kirk would continue to play key roles in the development of the alliance when they traveled back to the United States to prepare for the ABC-1 talks, which would be held in Washington DC.

ABC-1 Talks—29 January 1941–27 March 1941

The plenary session of the ABC-1 talks was held on 29 January 1941. The senior U.S. member at the talks was Army Major General S. D. Embick. RADM Ghormley was designated as the senior naval representative, with RADM Turner, the Navy's War Plans Officer, and CAPT Kirk, now the DNI, assisting.[279] CNO Stark stressed to the group that the security of the talks was of the utmost importance because, if word of them leaked out it would likely "cause a most serious delay in the coordination of our plans for war and a retarding effect on the passage of the Lend-Lease Bill," which was then making its way through Congress.[280] The purpose of the talks was to "determine the best methods by which the armed forces of the United States and the British Commonwealth...could defeat Germany and the Powers allied with her, should the United States be compelled to resort to war."[281] To this end, the participants were supposed to deter-

---

[276] "Stark Letter to Ghormley," 16 November 1940, *Stark Papers*; Harold Stark, ADM, USN, Chief of Naval Operations, Letter to Rear Admiral Robert Ghormley, USN,19 November 1940, *Stark Papers*.

[277] The U.S. accepted on 29 November 1940. For additional information see Reynolds, 184; Morison, *The Battle of the Atlantic*, 42-44.

[278] Morison, *The Battle of the Atlantic*, 44-45.

[279] *COMNAVEU Administrative History*, 9; Harold Stark, ADM, USN, Chief of Naval Operations, Letter to Rear Admiral Robert Ghormley, USN, 24 January 1941, *Strategic Planning*; "Minutes of the Plenary Meeting Held in Navy Department," 29 January 1941, *Strategic Planning*. Cited hereafter as "Plenary Meeting," 29 January 1941, Strategic Planning.

[280] Plenary Meeting," 29 January 1941, *Strategic Planning*.

[281] Department of the Navy, "Report on United States-British Staff Conversations," 27 March 1941, *Stark Papers*. Cited hereafter as "Report on U.S.-UK Staff Talks," 27 March 1941, *Stark Papers*.

mine the best means to coordinate U.S. and British efforts; delineate strategy and areas of responsibility; and work out command, control, communications, and intelligence issues.[282]

For the most part, the talks were very successful, although there were still some points of friction between the two prospective allies. While both countries agreed on the Germany-first strategy, planning to contain the Japanese in the Far East until the situation in Europe was stabilized, the British desired the U.S. to move its fleet to Singapore in the event of hostilities with Japan.[283] Predictably, the U.S. response was to reject this proposal and RADM Turner, who was highly distrustful of the British, drafted the response. Turner, wishing to think the worst of the British, believed they had been attempting to manipulate the U.S. fleet into protecting Singapore since the Ingersoll Mission 3 years previously.[284] Fortunately for the relationship between the two countries, Turner's personal views were kept within the U.S. delegation, although the U.S. had to reject the British proposal, given the need to maintain the U.S. fleet in Hawaii to protect America's West Coast and its own Far East possessions.

The other point of friction, which Turner also interpreted as a sign of British manipulation, occurred when it was discovered that the British delegation had reviewed with the British Ambassador some of the planning documents being discussed. The Ambassador then discussed them with the U.S. Secretary of State, who declined to address them and informed the Navy and War Departments of the situation. When this fact was discovered, the talks were immediately suspended and the U.S. delegation reiterated the terms of reference for the talks with their British counterparts, making it clear that these were military to military exchanges and, since no political commitments would be reached, these discussions should not include the policy arms of either government.[285]

Despite these problems, the talks resumed and ended successfully on 27 March 1941, and Roosevelt approved the recommendations made in April of that year.[286] What was the impact of the ABC-1 talks on intelligence sharing? The most immediate and tangible result was the establishment of Joint Missions: a standing British organization in Washington DC, and a parallel U.S. mission based in London. The purpose of these missions was to continue the planning

---

[282] Morison, *The Battle of the Atlantic*, 45; 48-49.

[283] Reynolds, 184-185; "British-United States Staff Conversations, 3rd Meeting Minutes," 3 February 1941, *Strategic Planning*, 1-5.

[284] "Minutes of Joint Meeting of Army and Navy Sections, United States Staff Committees, held in Navy Department Building," 13 February 1941, *Strategic Planning*, 1-2.

[285] "Minutes of Joint Meeting of Army and Navy Sections, United States Staff Committees, held in Navy Department Building," 19 February 1941, *Strategic Planning*.

[286] *COMNAVEU Administrative History*, 18.

efforts that had begun with the Standardization of Arms talks and to continue to work out the mechanics of cooperation in operational, intelligence, and communications matters.[287] The British Joint Staff Mission (JSM) was an effective tool for coordinating the allied war effort, although the British did attempt, with mixed results, to use the mission as a means of influencing the development of U.S. military capabilities and operations.[288] On intelligence matters, the main agreement reached during the ABC-1 staff talks was that all existing intelligence organizations would continue to act independently but they were to

> maintain close liaison with each other in order to ensure the full and prompt exchange of pertinent information concerning war operations. Intelligence [would be] established not only through the Military Missions but also between all echelons of command in the field with respect to matters which affect their operations.[289]

By May 1941, a Joint Intelligence Committee (JIC) was established as a component of the JSM and the NID stood up a new branch, NID-18, to serve as the naval component of the JSM JIC and to conduct liaison with ONI.[290] Hinsley states that soon after the establishment of these missions, SIGINT sharing began to take place on a regular basis, which, given the sensitivity of the material

---

[287] Hinsley, *British Intel* vol. 1, 313; Bath, 63-63.

[288] Smith, *Ultra-Magic Deals*, 68-69. The British were continually frustrated by the lack of inter-service organizations in the U.S. military, since it created a situation where they were forced to negotiate everything with the separate services. The JSM consistently made recommendations to the U.S. Departments of War and the Navy concerning ways they could better organize themselves for war, in essence, to become more like the British. For example, the British recommended the U.S. military branches form a JIC-like organization to coordinate intelligence policy and create an inter-service board to coordinate the development and acquisition of radar technology across the services. Both suggestions were flatly rejected by both the War and Navy Departments. Without the pressure of actual war to spur on cooperation between the services, there was little incentive to overcome bureaucratic rivalries and suggestions from the British, even at this stage in the relationship between the two countries, were treated warily. For additional information see Smith, *Ultra-Magic Deals*, 69; British Joint Staff Mission, "Proposal to Setup an Inter-services R.D.F. Committee in North America," 26 August 1941, *Strategic Planning*, 1-2; U.S. Navy Secretary for Collaboration, Letter to British Joint Staff Mission, 18 November 1941, *Strategic Planning*.

[289] "Report on U.S.-UK Staff Talks," 27 March 1941, *Stark Papers*. Bath contends that the British actually advocated stronger wording for this section of the agreement, desiring full intelligence sharing, not sharing limited to operational matters. He also notes that implementation of this policy was uneven. For example, U.S. attachés did not receive word to cooperate with their British counterparts until November of 1941. For additional information see Bath, 54-55.

[290] Francis Hally Hinsley and others, *British Intelligence in the Second World War: Its Influence on Strategy and Operations 2* (New York: Cambridge University Press, 1981), 47, cited hereafter as Hinsley, *British Intel*, vol. 2; Hinsley, *British Intel* vol. 1, 313; MacLachlan, 219-220; Bath, 64.

involved, is a good indicator that information from other sources was being shared as well.[291]

The U.S. naval mission to England was placed under RADM Ghormley's charge and the new U.S. naval attaché, CAPT Charles P. Lockwood, assumed duties as both the attaché and as Ghormley's Chief of Staff.[292] This staff, which would form the nucleus of what would later become the Commander, Naval Forces Europe Staff, contained significantly more naval observers than had been in England in the past and, to avoid tensions, "great emphasis was placed on picking officers who would be discreet and cooperative in working with the British."[293] The flow of information from the British, established by the Bailey Committee, continued to flourish and material that was previously held closely was now open to the Americans, given that the British now had formal agreements and the Lend-Lease program to assuage their doubts about U.S. cooperation.[294] Processing this increased amount of technical and intelligence information became an issue, however, and a division of labor was established whereby the "Naval Attaché served as the channel for supplying intelligence of enemy organization, operations, and plans....Operational intelligence became increasingly a function of the staff of the Special Naval Observer [Ghormley]."[295] One of the most tangible benefits of the exchanges once the U.S. mission was established was in the area of imagery intelligence (IMINT). Ghormley was granted permission to have an officer observe British aerial photographic reconnaissance and imagery interpretation operations. The officer assigned to this task, Lieutenant Commander Robert S. Quackenbush, was highly impressed with British capabilities in this area and his efforts led to the establishment of the first U.S. imagery interpreter school in September 1941.[296] While this cooperation in IMINT was significant, the start of U.S.-UK SIGINT cooperation can also be traced to this period, although this major achievement was overshadowed by the

---

[291] Hinsley, *British Intel* vol. 2, 55. Hinsley states that, when the JSM JIC was stood up, the common perspective of the British was that, "Washington...had little to offer, and...closer contacts with the United States intelligence organizations left the British authorities in no doubt that it would have little to offer for many months." This was not an entirely fair assessment, given the U.S. success against the Japanese Purple code and the generally superior state of U.S. intelligence on Japan, but it does give insight into the British mindset at the time, which was chauvinistic and completely focused on the European situation. For additional information see Hinsley, *British Intel*, vol. 1, 314.

[292] Bath, 56.

[293] *COMNAVEU Administrative History*, 11, 14; Alan Goodrich Kirk, CAPT, USN, Director of Naval Intelligence, Letter to Rear Admiral Walter S. Anderson, USN, 27 March 1941, *Kirk Papers*.

[294] 2 Bath, 56.

[295] *COMNAVEU Administrative History*, 108. There would be 103 assistant U.S. naval attachés in England by September 1941. For additional information see *COMNAVEU Administrative History*, 34.

[296] Packard, 179-180; Dorwart, *Conflict of Duty*, 154-155.

high-level ABC-1 staff talks which were occurring at the same time. Although much has been written on SIGINT cooperation between the two countries, the origins of that cooperation are worth reviewing as they demonstrate a major step in the establishment of trust and mutual respect between the two allies.

American Approach—The Sinkov Mission
February 1941

BGEN Strong had made the initial offer on SIGINT cooperation with the British during the 31 August 1940 session of the Standardization of Arms Talks. Soon after making the offer, in September 1940, U.S. Army cryptologists working under the great William Friedman would complete their successful reverse engineering of the cipher machine used to encrypt the Japanese diplomatic code (Purple). The decrypted intelligence from this source was known as MAGIC.[297] Although he disagreed with Strong's making the offer, Ghormley met with RADM Godfrey and Sir Stewart Menzies on 22 October 1940 to begin working out the details of the SIGINT technical exchange. The deal had not yet been approved in the U.S.; however, on 23 October, Secretary of the Navy Knox and Secretary of War Stimson agreed to the exchange and obtained approval from Roosevelt sometime in late October or early November. The proposed list of items to be exchanged by the Americans included copies of the Japanese Red and Purple cipher machines, the main German diplomatic code, some of the Japanese diplomatic codes, and some of the Italian and Mexican codes which the U.S. had decrypted. The main resistance for this exchange came from the Navy's cryptanalytic branch, OP-20-G, although the Navy agreed to send two of its personnel on the exchange mission.[298] There was also resistance to the exchange in Great Britain as SIGINT was one of the few intelligence items that had been off-limits to the Americans. Concerns about U.S. security and Churchill's desire to use ULTRA intelligence, the information derived from the successful decryption of German messages encrypted using Enigma, as a bargaining chip in British negotiations with the U.S. government, were the main factors on the British side inhibiting exchange on this topic.[299]

---

[297] Erskine, 58-59, 69; Smith, *Ultra-Magic Deals*, 34-35, 44-46.
[298] Erskine, 59; Smith, *Ultra-Magic Deals*, 48-49, 50-54.
[299] Smith, *Ultra-Magic Deals*, 30, 59-62.

Despite reservations on both sides, the U.S. mission departed for London in January 1941, around the time the ABC-1 talks were beginning. Although William Friedman was supposed to be in charge of the mission, he had suffered a nervous breakdown earlier in the month and leadership of the four-man mission devolved to Abraham Sinkov, who, with the temporary rank of Army Captain, was the senior man on the team.[300] While the specifics of what was exchanged during the Sinkov team's visit to the GC&CS at Bletchley Park has been a matter of some debate for many years, recent scholarship has demonstrated that both the U.S. and Great Britain benefited greatly from the exchange and its ultimate outcome was an increase in SIGINT cooperation between the two countries.[301]

The Sinkov Mission arrived in England on 7 February 1941. The dates of the mission's stay in Great Britain are somewhat unclear, but the team most likely made its visit to Bletchley Park sometime later in February and probably returned to the U.S. by 20 March 1941.[302] The mission was cordially received by Denniston at the GC&CS and the British were most appreciative of the American's willingness to provide them with the two Purple machines and the information on the various foreign codes they were willing to share. Although the British did not have Enigma machines they could spare for an exchange at this point, they did provide the U.S. with a wiring diagram for constructing their own Enigma machine, although it would be many months before the Americans would be able

---

[300] Baer, 54-55; Erskine, 60; Lewin, 114.

[301] The main controversy surrounding the exchange concerns accusations made by CDR Laurence Safford of the Navy's OP-20-G, who contended there was a deal made before the Sinkov team left for England whereby the U.S. would provide England a copy of the Purple encrypting machine in exchange for a copy of an Enigma machine. No scholar has ever found evidence of such an agreement and it is doubtful one existed. For Safford, the U.S. had given up its "crown jewels" by handing over two Purple machines to the British and had, in his mind, nothing to show for it. Much of the controversy also stems from the fact that, in his official report, Sinkov did not reveal the full extent of what the British shared with him concerning Enigma and the early British computers (bombes) used for decryption because he had sworn an oath by which he had agreed to provide this information only to the Army G-2 and the Navy's DNI. Recently declassified documents demonstrate that those who participated in the mission and senior leadership in the Navy and War Departments felt the exchange of information was equitable, further undercutting Safford's assertions. British desire to monopolize ULTRA intelligence, however, was a source of friction between the two countries and probably was a factor that colored Safford's recollection of the time and his distrust of the British. For additional information see Erskine 60-66, 72; Smith, *Ultra-Magic Deals*, 56-62, 75-76; Aldrich, 77-78.

[302] The period of the visit to Bletchley Park was quite short. Most of the team's time in England was spent waiting for transportation back to America. For additional information see Erskine, 67, 74.

to successfully interpret the instructions they received.[303] While the Sinkov team was not allowed to see any of the actual intelligence derived from ULTRA, they were told, according to one of the team members, U.S. Navy Ensign Prescott Currier, about "the latest techniques applied to the solution of Enigma and in the operations of the Bombes [early British computers]."[304] In addition to information on Enigma, the Sinkov team received a detailed briefing on the organization of the GC&CS; information on the location and operation of Royal Air Force and Army intercept and DF capabilities; various German, Italian, Russian, Italian, and Japanese codes; and training materials.[305] Given the depth and scope of the highly sensitive information shared, the mission's main result was to create an atmosphere of trust that would enable greater intelligence cooperation over the course of 1941, particularly in the Far Eastern theater.

---

[303] The U.S. sent a number of requests to the British to clarify the instructions they were given concerning the construction of an Enigma machine. While the British were somewhat reluctant to answer questions about Enigma for security reasons, the unreliability of the mails was another factor. Denniston tried to answer questions in November 1941 but his answers were lost. Most likely, Safford saw this delay as another indicator of British truculence, contributing to his negative view of British assistance prior to the war. For additional information see Budiansky, 54-57; Smith, *Ultra-Magic Deals*, 75-76; Bray, xx-xxi.

[304] Smith, *Ultra-Magic Deals*, 76. For additional information see Hinsley, *British Intel*, vol. 1, 313; Bath, 57-58.

[305] Erskine, 63; Bath 57-58.

Chapter 7

THE LIMITS OF EXCHANGE
MARCH 1941-DECEMBER 1941

The ABC-1 staff talks marked a tipping point in the relationship between the U.S. and Great Britain. America was still, officially, a neutral but it was evident to the world that new policies, such as Lend-Lease and more aggressive patrolling of the Western Atlantic by the U.S. Navy, strongly favored the British. Though much had been done to improve operational and intelligence cooperation between the two countries in preparation for the eventual U.S. entry into the war, the British still sought additional ways through which they could tie the U.S. more closely to their war effort. Intelligence remained an area where that greater cooperation could be forged without attracting undue attention from Roosevelt's isolationist critics. Intelligence cooperation also became increasingly necessary as the Far East situation deteriorated and as the U.S. Navy transitioned to convoying and protecting shipping in the Western Atlantic. From the conclusion of the ABC-1 talks until the Pearl Harbor attacks, the British would continue to put forward initiatives designed to encourage closer cooperation between the two governments and their navies.

Exchanges in the Far East

Following the successful ABC-1 talks, which established the Atlantic-first strategy for the allies, the UK attempted to forge a strategic policy for the Far East through a conference between American, British, and Dutch (ABD) officials. Although a plan was drafted on 27 April 1941, it was rejected by both the U.S. Army and Navy in June of that year.[306] As had been the problem since early 1939, the British did not have the forces required to protect their Far East possessions and had put their hope in the fact the U.S. would come to their aid in that theater when war came. For the U.S., burdened with its own security obligations in the Orient, this expectation was unreasonable and unrealistic. While U.S. planners believed they probably had the capability to defend Hawaii, Singapore, and the Philippines, they would be stretched thin and they would be unable to generate or sustain a substantive offensive in the opening stages of the war. This strategy would be in strong contradiction to Mahanian principles.[307] Even though an agreement was eventually reached, it amounted

---

[306] Morison, *Rising Sun*, 55.
[307] Morison, *Rising Sun*, 53-55.

to little more than a nebulous statement on the part of the signatories to cooperate with one another if war came.[308]

Despite this lack of cooperation on a strategic and operational level, both the U.S. and the UK still sought ways to increase exchanges between their intelligence organizations in the theater. Historically, exchanges in the Far Eastern theater had been relatively informal, primarily at the attaché-to-attaché level.[309] This situation began to change in October 1940, when, as previously discussed, an agreement was reached through the Joint Bailey Committee to exchange liaison officers between Great Britain's China Fleet and the U.S. Asiatic Fleet.[310] This was still a limited means of exchanging information, however, and officials in British intelligence felt more could be done to engage the U.S. in this theater. Plans were made to undertake initiatives that would increase cooperation in the Far East.

The first move toward greater cooperation in the Orient came on the heels of the Sinkov Mission when, in March 1941, the British DNI, RADM Godfrey, authorized an exchange of SIGINT information between the British Far East Combined Bureau (FECB) in Singapore and the U.S. cryptologists at Station CAST in the Philippines. By 14 March, the FECB had given the U.S. partial solutions to a Japanese Army transport code and a cipher used by their Air Force. By 23 March the FECB was given approval to accept two U.S. Army cryptologists as liaison officers.[311] Starting in May 1941, the U.S. Navy and the FECB worked out the details of their exchange, which was significant. Lieutenant Jefferson Dennison, the officer-in-charge at Station CAST, traveled to Singapore in April or early May to explore the possibility of greater cooperation. The Navy was still trying to break the main Japanese Fleet code, JN-25B, but was having only limited success. To foster good will and increase cooperation, the British provided all the work they had done on JN-25B and the addition of the code groups they had recovered was a significant help to the Americans, who likewise provided the work they had done on the code.[312]

Following Dennison's visit, in May 1941, Commander Malcolm Burnett of the Royal Navy arrived at Corregidor to work out the final details of a SIGINT-sharing arrangement between the FECB and Station CAST. While the British were farther along in their code breaking efforts, they lacked reliable access to traffic

---

[308] Bath, 156-157.

[309] Dorwart, *Conflict of Duty*, 133-134; Bath, 135.

[310] Bath, 155-159.

[311] Smith, Ultra-Magic Deals, 78; Antony Best, *Britain, Japan, and Pearl Harbor: Avoiding War in East Asia, 1936-1941* (New York: Routledge, 1995), 146.

[312] Smith, *Ultra-Magic Deals*, 78; Erskine, 63-64.

emanating from Japanese home waters and were eager to obtain the greater volume of signals the U.S. could provide them for analysis.[313] A formal agreement was reached whereby a special radio circuit would be used to share information using a one-time pad code for the security of the transmission.[314] Hardcopy traffic and detailed analyses were sent using a regularly scheduled flight from Manila to Singapore.[315] Given the success of these exchanges, the U.S. Army attaché in London, in late May 1941, made a request to the British government, on behalf of the War Department, requesting a full exchange of intelligence information in the Far East. During a 6 June 1941 meeting of the British JIC, the British reached a decision to share all their intelligence in the Far East, except their SIS and SOE operations, with the Americans.[316] Although this was a significant offer on the part of the British, it was a difficult policy to implement, despite its having been enacted at the request of the American government. As Richard Aldrich has observed, the U.S. had no comparable inter-service intelligence organization that the British could deal with, so every agreement needed to be worked out between individual departments of the U.S. government.[317] Alan Bath has also noted that the U.S. was slow to respond to Far East initiatives as the threat there seemed less urgent and many in leadership positions were still wary of any British desire to maintain their colonial empire.[318] Both Aldrich and Bath are correct in pointing out that perennial problems in the relationship between the two countries existed as late as the summer of 1941 and continued to work against better cooperation on both operational and intelligence matters.

The Godfrey Visit—May-June 1941

In parallel with the effort to improve intelligence cooperation in the Far East, the JIC in London was still interested in ways to improve the cooperation and coordination of U.S. and UK intelligence in the Atlantic theater. To this end, Godfrey was dispatched on a mission from the JIC to assess the state of U.S. intelligence and, as Donald MacLachlan has stated, "to persuade the Americans to pool their intelligence with ours [the British], to adopt those of our methods which had been proved by nearly two years' experience and to accept all we were prepared

---

313 Smith, *Ultra-Magic Deals*, 79; Worth, 106-107
314 Stripp, 148; Aldrich, 80; Smith, *Ultra-Magic Deals*, 82; Worth, 105.
315 Smith, *Ultra-Magic Deals*, 82.
316 Best, 146-147; Aldrich, 80; Bath, 163-164.
317 Aldrich, 80-81.
318 Bath, 159.

to offer."[319] Others in the British JIC were not so sanguine about a closer relationship, given they did not respect the quality of U.S. intelligence and felt little more could be gained from further cooperation.[320] Still, a mini-JIC had been established in the British embassy under the JSM and Godfrey felt there was great potential for increased sharing of intelligence through that organization, particularly if he could convince the Americans to set up a similar council for the coordination of U.S. intelligence activities.[321]

Godfrey had suspected he would find the U.S. farther behind on intelligence matters than the British. Even so, he was taken aback by what he actually found. He was given a tour of ONI by his old associate, CAPT Kirk, now DNI, and came away unimpressed, feeling that ONI's lack of access to naval planning efforts had made it largely irrelevant.[322] While seeing some bright spots in the areas of decrypting Japanese codes and their penetration of the South American and Vichy French North African targets, Godfrey could find little to praise about U.S. intelligence. The litany of defects he reported to the JIC in London included his perception that, for many in the U.S. government, intelligence just meant security and counterintelligence work; general situation reports were highly valued but tactical and operational intelligence were not; there was no joint intelligence production, which led to duplicative effort and conflicting reporting; intelligence was done for intelligence's sake since there was no interface between intelligence and planning; hard, in-depth analysis was lacking and there was no means of grading intelligence products; and the U.S. possessed no SIS, propaganda, SOE, or economic warfare branch equivalents.[323]

Hoping to improve the situation, Godfrey attempted to be helpful by providing the War and Navy Departments with a series of memos on subjects such as the grading of intelligence reports, topographic intelligence, security of sources, the handling of special intelligence between the U.S. and the UK, prisoner-of-war intelligence, the handling of ciphers, and the functions of the NID's Operational Intelligence Center (OIC).[324] Godfrey also recommended to the services that they form a U.S. JIC to coordinate their intelligence efforts, which would act as a sin-

---

[319] MacLachlan, 217.

[320] MacLachlan, 222-223; Hinsley, *British Intel* vol. 1, 314.

[321] Bradley F. Smith, "Admiral Godfrey's Mission to America, June/July 1941," *Intelligence and National Security* 1, no. 3 (September, 1986): 441-442, 447. Cited hereafter as Smith, "ADM Godfrey's Mission." Smith's article contains the complete text of Godfrey's post-trip report as an appendix.

[322] Dorwart, *Conflict of Duty*, 148; Joseph E. Persico, *Roosevelt's Secret War* (New York: Random House, 2001), 81-82; Smith, Ultra-Magic Deals, 31-32; Bath, 60-61.

[323] Smith, "ADM Godfrey's Mission," 445-447, 449; Smith, *Ultra-Magic Deals*, 31-32, 71.

[324] Smith, "ADM Godfrey's Mission," 448-449.

gle point through which the British could gain access to U.S. intelligence. As could be expected, Godfrey's helpful suggestions were perceived quite differently by the services, who were, uncharacteristically, in complete agreement that they did not desire or need a central intelligence organization in America. COL Raymond Lee, the U.S. military attaché in London, received the official Army G-2 rejection of Godfrey's proposal for a U.S. JIC on 26 June 1941. Attached to this was a personal letter from the G-2, Colonel Hayes Knone, which made it clear that the Army's attitude toward the proposal was "we are not going to copy British organization and procedure[,]...[w]e are not convinced that such a central clearing house and assimilating center are needed [, and]...[t]he British have not been successful, so far, in this war; why should they advise us?"[325]

This reaction, predicated on both the desire to be treated as an equal of Great Britain and on inter-service rivalry, was not limited to the Army. In addition to pitching his idea for a JIC, Godfrey and his protégé, Commander Ian Fleming,[326] also worked closely with William Donovan and William Stephenson to develop the ideas that would form Donovan's famous memorandum to Roosevelt recommending the creation of a central intelligence organization for America. Godfrey even met with Roosevelt and discussed the idea of a central intelligence authority with him.[327] Kirk was aware of this meeting and, most likely through his personal relationship with Donovan, was also aware of Godfrey's role in advocating a central intelligence organization. Kirk, displaying the attitude of his Service at attempts by the British to meddle in U.S. affairs, made no attempt to hide his displeasure with Godfrey when the British DNI paid Kirk a courtesy call prior to his return to England.[328] While the depth and breadth of the intelligence exchanges between the two countries would continue to grow after Godfrey's visit, the U.S. position, at least at the higher levels of the military services, was that advice from Great Britain on how to conduct their affairs was not desired and would be met with resentment.

---

[325] Leutze, *London Journal.* journal entry for 26 June 1941. Godfrey must have been received quite cordially by the two Services, however, who probably politely told him they would consider his suggestions. In his official report, Godfrey optimistically predicted that "the U.S. authorities are willing to gain, if not be guided by, our experience over the past two years." For additional information see Smith, "ADM Godfrey's Mission," 449.

[326] Commander Ian Fleming would later gain great notoriety as the author of the James Bond novels.

[327] Beesly, *Very Special Intelligence,* 113; Smith, "ADM Godfrey's Mission," 443, 447-448; Beesly, *Very Special Admiral,* 181-183; Dorwart, *Conflict of Duty,* 231.

[328] MacLachlan, 231.

Operational Intelligence Cooperation—April 1941—November 1941

From April 1941 to November 1941, events in the Atlantic clearly indicate that the U.S. had abandoned its neutral stance in favor of alliance with Great Britain. As military preparations for this alliance were ongoing, U.S. security interests prompted Roosevelt to take actions that were decidedly pro-British and, while some of these actions met with popular outcry, public opinion was moving toward Roosevelt's view. In April 1941, the U.S. began basing forces in Greenland, to aid in the maintenance of security patrols. By this time all U.S. ship sightings of U-boats were passed back to the Admiralty through ALUSNA London. Although this information was not timely, it still assisted the British in developing their operational intelligence (OPINTEL) picture and was just the sort of intelligence cooperation they had hoped to obtain from the Americans when they first began to press for a closer relationship.[329] In June 1941, Churchill pressed Sir Stewart Menzies to ease the restrictions on the dissemination of U-boat Enigma decrypts and, while the British would be slow to act on this, the U.S. did begin receiving intelligence derived from this source.[330] Additionally, by July 1941, the U.S. and the UK routinely shared intelligence derived from HF/DF sites.[331] As the summer progressed, the relationship would become closer still. In July 1941, the U.S. would take over the defense of Iceland, relieving British forces of the need to perform that duty. During the Atlantic Conference between Roosevelt and Churchill in August, one of the substantive agreements reached was a policy for the conduct of convoy operations and areas of responsibility for the two countries, giving further incentive to share intelligence on German naval movements. U.S. Navy encounters with German U-boats, such as the Greer Incident, inflamed public opinion against the Germans enough that Roosevelt was able to advise Germany and Italy to keep their warships out of waters under U.S. protection. By the time the *Reuben James* was torpedoed by a U-boat in late October 1941, Congress was prepared to amend the neutrality laws in ways that made the alliance with the British a reality in fact, if not on paper.[332]

Against this backdrop, two additional visits were made in an effort to further increase intelligence collaboration between the two countries. To reciprocate the Sinkov Mission, Commander Alistair Denniston, the Director of GC&CS, visited the United States to discuss ways to enhance SIGINT cooperation. Although his efforts to establish new, official frameworks for collaboration met with no success, the Denniston visit did have a positive outcome. He completely impressed

---

[329] Smith, *Ultra-Magic Deals*, 75-76.

[330] Hinsley, *British Intel*, vol. 2, 55.

[331] Bray, xxi.

[332] Morison, *The Battle of the Atlantic*, 69-71, 75-76, 78-81.

U.S. cryptologists with whom he came in contact through his personality and technical acumen. He began a personal friendship with William Friedman and others, which greatly assisted in the future development of the closer ties between U.S.-UK SIGINT organizations that developed once the U.S. entered the war.[333]

The second visit of significance was that led by Commander Arthur McCollum, U.S. Navy, from August through October 1941. McCollum's trip was to reciprocate the visit the U.S. had received from Godfrey earlier in the year.[334] The trip was significant in that it showed that the tensions that existed within the relationship were still prevalent on the eve of the U.S. entry into the war. For example, even though McCollum got along well with his British hosts on a personal level and was given a great deal of access to the NID, he did not have a very high opinion of British abilities. When asked years later about whether he had seen Room 39, the OIC's main plotting room, McCollum responded to an interviewer that he "may have seen it, I don't know. Like everything British, you know, you get the impression that it's not very well organized, that it's rather diffused, but it does work."[335] McCollum also had little confidence in British assessments on Japan, believing the British lack of focus on the Far East problem significantly inhibited their ability to do substantive work on that country.[336] As McCollum continued his exploration of the NID, he realized that he was being prevented from seeing some aspects of the organization, particularly how decrypted COMINT was being integrated by the NID. He confronted Godfrey on the issue and uncharacteristically, he was told

> "Well, you know, McCollum, that's a very difficult thing to do
> because we don't control that. I couldn't possibly offer anything of
> that sort because I really don't have any control over it." I said, "Well,
> Admiral, who does?" and he said, "Damned if I know," which of
> course was ridiculous.[337]

---

[333] Smith, *Ultra-Magic Deals*, 89; Bath, 62-63.

[334] *McCollum Reminiscences*, 338. McCollum eventually retired as Rear Admiral from the Naval Service and his reminiscences are filled with many frank insights on the functioning of the U.S. Navy during this period. While it may seem odd that the Navy would reciprocate Godfrey's visit with that from a CDR, McCollum was not originally supposed to be the senior man on the mission. Given the vagaries of travel during this period, the senior member of the team took a different flight from McCollum, a flight which crashed over England, killing all aboard. Unfortunately for McCollum, who was in charge of the Japan Desk at ONI, he had been given only the vaguest notions of what the goals of the mission were. For additional information see *McCollum Reminiscences*, 339-342.

[335] *McCollum Reminiscences*, 343.

[336] *McCollum Reminiscences*, 350.

[337] *McCollum Reminiscences*, 344.

Godfrey's main concern was most likely security, once again showing the British distrust of the U.S. on this issue. While information was being exchanged on the mechanics of decrypting Japanese communications and while the U.S. was receiving sanitized intelligence derived from ULTRA at this stage, raw intelligence from that source was still closely held by the British.[338] McCollum would fortuitously encounter an old friend after his meeting with Godfrey, one who had access to the highest levels of the Admiralty. The next day McCollum was called in to see the First Sea Lord, ADM Sir Dudley Pound, who told him that Godfrey had been instructed to hold nothing back from him. After this, McCollum was given full access to the OIC and was able to see how proficient the British were at using all-source intelligence fusion to maintain the tactical picture in the Atlantic and engage in predictive analysis of U-boat operations. McCollum would bring this valuable information back to the U.S. Navy and would use it to set up the first pilot program that would later become the Fleet Intelligence Center, for the Pacific Fleet in Hawaii.[339]

Although the British had desired a system of collaborative OPINTEL centers on both sides of the Atlantic almost from the inception of the OIC, it was never a real possibility given the fundamentally different ways each navy viewed intelligence and, consequently, had organized their intelligence services to meet those views. Eventually the U.S. Fleet commanders saw a need for an OPINTEL capability and, rather than going to ONI for this service, they chose to create their own intelligence fusion centers within their staff organizations.[340] Although initially far more limited in capability than the British OIC, these Fleet Intelligence Centers would, due to the pressure of war, eventually grow to rival their British counterpart.

---

[338] Smith, *Ultra-Magic Deals*, 86-87; Aldrich, 81.
[339] *McCollum Reminiscences*, 330-331, 345-346, 353.
[340] Beesly, *Very Special Intelligence*, 112-113; Packard, 216

Chapter 8

EVALUATION:
SUCCESS OF THE BRITISH EFFORT

The British aggressively used a number of highly effective tactics to secure a closer intelligence relationship with the U.S. prior to the U.S.'s actually entering the war. These approaches took place on many levels and through many venues as part of a comprehensive, although not necessarily well coordinated, plan on the part of the British to draw the U.S. into World War II as their ally. Although the U.S. may have been predisposed to aid the British, given their common interests, it is unlikely the U.S. would have drawn as close to the British as they did in the period from 1938 to 1941 were it not for persistent British overtures.

As the U.S. progressed toward supporting Britain in the war, intelligence exchanges between the two countries became commonplace. Although increased cooperation was consistently hampered by tensions and animosities, by the time the U.S. entered the war, cooperation in the area of intelligence, particularly naval intelligence, was well beyond anything anyone would have imagined possible in 1939. Although U.S. decisionmakers in the Navy hierarchy—Roosevelt, Knox, and Stark—were predisposed to aid the British, because they clearly saw it was in the U.S. national interest to do so, they were also very cautious. Even though they were receptive to British overtures, the initiation of cooperative ventures was difficult given domestic political constraints and the U.S. desire, especially among military officials, to be treated as equals by the British. Given this reluctance on the part of the American policymakers and senior military officials, it is highly unlikely that the level of intelligence cooperation attained between the two navies in the interwar period would have been as extensive and wide-ranging as it became, were it not for repeated British initiatives designed to advance that purpose. By gambling well with the most significant bargaining chips available to them—their technical advances, intelligence resources, and war experience—the British secured a "special relationship" with the United States in matters of intelligence, a relationship that still brings substantial benefits to both sides.

Lessons for The U.S. Intelligence Community

If the rationale for intelligence sharing can be reduced to a cost-benefit calculation whereby countries seek to mitigate weaknesses in their intelligence capability by seeking to arrange a limited partnership with a state or group that possesses complementary capabilities,[341] it is in practice a highly complex process. A state must determine its "potential partner's reliability, stability, and potential durability," and must work out how the intelligence will be exchanged, the limits of that exchange, and what security protocols will be enacted to protect the information provided.[342] A country cannot assume that another government operates in the same way and must correctly ascertain the factors and individuals who truly influence policy before beginning the negotiations necessary to effect the exchange.[343]

The most serious risk in intelligence sharing may be the exposure of sources and methods, but there are other potential dangers to sharing intelligence. These include the chance that intelligence given to one country will find its way to a third, potentially hostile, state; a propensity for circular reporting; increased pressure to share intelligence in other areas; and the risk that disclosure of the intelligence sharing could be politically harmful to the governments engaged in the exchanges.[344] The potential benefits of exchange are significant, however. The largest benefit is that intelligence cooperation can provide needed intelligence that may be unobtainable otherwise. Cooperation may expand a country's readily available collection targets, or it may be a way to employ collection technologies that would otherwise be unavailable to one of the exchange partners.[345] Another major benefit may be in the area of influence. A state may provide intelligence to another country in the hope of influencing that country to act in a certain way. Cooperation may also be used as a way to engage another state diplomatically in a situation where no strong diplomatic ties exist.[346]

As in the post-Cold War period, the U.S., in the 20th century interwar timeframe, experienced a multiplicity of new threats at a time when the resources devoted to intelligence were declining. This produced a situation whereby intelligence exchange had to be considered by resource managers as the most efficient and effective means of addressing these requirements.[347] In one observer's view, during periods of heightened crisis, the American public is much more willing to tolerate associations that would be questionable during a more stable

---

[341] Gideon Doron, "The Vagaries of Intelligence Sharing: The Political Imbalance," *International Journal of Intelligence and Counterintelligence* 6, no. 1 (Summer 1993): 135.

[342] Doron, 135.

[343] Doron, 141-142.

[344] Jeffrey T. Richelson, "The Calculus of Intelligence Cooperation," *International Journal of Intelligence and Counterintelligence* 4, no. 3 (Fall 1990): 315-318.

[345] Richelson, 311-315.

[346] Richelson, 314-315.

[347] James J. Wirtz, "Constraints on Intelligence Collaboration: The Domestic Dimension," *International Journal of Intelligence and Counterintelligence* 6, no. 1 (Spring 1993): 86.

period.[348] The conditions in the interwar period were marked by increasing instability. While the primary reaction from the American public to this instability was isolationism, Americans became increasingly more tolerant of a foreign policy tilt toward Great Britain once the war began to impact U.S. interests.

For both parties examined in this study, the risks of intelligence sharing were significant. The major obstacles to closer cooperation for U.S. policymakers during the critical summer of 1940 were determining whether England would survive the war and whether they could be trusted to keep the nascent intelligence relationship secret. The main factor the British had to overcome was their concern about lax U.S. counterintelligence practices. Despite these concerns, the benefits were considerable. Given the success of the British effort in securing the "special relationship" with the U.S. in intelligence cooperation in the interwar period, some lessons can be drawn from the experience:

1. Be prepared to quickly capitalize on a shared crisis

The British were able to rapidly exploit instances when the sense of crisis among U.S. decisionmakers was highest. During periods of higher tension, countries are more willing to seek solutions to their problems that would have been unacceptable during times of greater stability. For example, the British had attempted to engage the U.S. in a closer relationship on Japan policy following the abortive London Naval Conference of 1935, but they met with little success until the *Panay* Incident in December 1937 heightened U.S. concerns about the Japanese threat. After the *Panay* Incident, the British immediately engaged U.S. decisionmakers once again and secured the Ingersoll Mission for their efforts. Similarly, British overtures to the U.S. in the period following the start of the war in September 1939 met with little success. The defeat of Belgium, Holland, and France, however, created a sense of crisis in the U.S., one the British exploited to secure Donovan's visit to England and U.S. participation in the Standardization of Arms Talks. The Bailey Committee Report shows that the British were ready to capitalize on initiatives like the Standardization of Arms Talks. The report demonstrates that the British prepared well for these opportunities, clearly defining their goals, the types of information they wished to exchange, and the methods by which those exchanges would take place, factors that decisionmakers must take into account before engaging in cooperative intelligence ventures.

---

[348] Wirtz, 93-94.

2. Be prepared to give something of value without expecting reciprocation

The Tizard Mission is the most powerful example of this principle, and many of the British overtures in the period before the U.S. entered the war could be characterized in this fashion. Individuals like RADM Godfrey and Henry Tizard correctly assessed that providing the U.S. with information on a non-reciprocal basis was the key to unlocking U.S. good will and cooperation. The extent and depth of the technical information the British were prepared to provide to the U.S. gratis had a tremendous impact on U.S. decisionmakers, positively disposing them to greater cooperation on technical matters. Similarly, the British willingness to share information on the German magnetic mine and to give the U.S. preferential treatment in examining war damage, all done with no reciprocation from the U.S., were major factors influencing CAPT Kirk's advocacy of the British position. While the impact was not immediate, major exchanges, like those conducted by the Tizard Mission, made it clear to U.S. decisionmakers that the benefits of cooperation with the British outweighed the risks. For the U.S., the exchanges were principally a means of compensating for weakness in their technological development and intelligence capabilities, while for the British, the exchanges were principally a means of influencing U.S. policy in the interwar period.

3. Know your target

While it is true that some in the British hierarchy, even Churchill, may not have clearly understood the high degree to which domestic political considerations weighed on decisionmaking by U.S. policymakers, others, like Stephenson, were keen observers of the American political scene. They had correctly ascertained who the key decisionmakers were in the U.S. government and how best to influence them. Today and in the future, a considered decision to share intelligence with a state that may be wary of U.S. intentions depends on fully understanding who the top decisionmakers are, how they are predisposed toward cooperation, and who may have influence with those decisionmakers if direct access is not achievable or would be counterproductive. In the present study, Stephenson's choice of Donovan as an interlocutor for British interests appears brilliant. Donovan was a man outside the administration, yet he was respected by key decisionmakers and was on friendly terms with influential cabinet members who were already predisposed to cooperate with Great Britain. Since Donovan had access and was persuasive, the British cultivated him at every opportunity, ensuring he carried their message to the highest levels of the American government.

4. Engagement attempts should be multilevel and multifarious

The number and types of engagement attempts will depend largely on what is at stake in securing a closer relationship with the target country. For the British, the stakes were national survival; consequently their engagement attempts took place on as many levels as possible, using a variety of forums. The military-to-military intelligence exchanges characterized here were just one element of a multilevel effort to secure U.S. cooperation in the war. Even within this limited arena, the British sought to engage at any level they could. From the low-level observer missions, through the ALUSNA London office, and on to the office of the CNO and the Secretary of the Navy, the British sent a relatively consistent message that they wanted U.S. support and they were willing to openly share their secrets to obtain it. The types of exchanges they were willing to engage in are also significant. They demonstrated a willingness to share many different types of information—technical, operational, and political, for example—reasoning that the more varied the forums of exchange, the more likely they were to positively influence a key decisionmaker. In less desperate circumstances than those faced by the British, it is doubtful that any country would engage in such a wide-ranging exchange of secret information.

5. Openness and candor are essential for building trust

Granted, this is an obvious point, but one which was vital to establishing the cooperative relationship between the U.S. and the UK. Kirk, Ghormley, Donovan, and numerous others marveled at the openness and frankness of the British in discussing their war situation and in the provision of secret information. Many were looking for any sign that the British were once again poised to treat the Americans as junior partners, which had aggravated many during the Great War, as they felt the British had often been less than candid on many issues. Even Kirk, who has been seen by some as very pro-British, due to his advocacy of greater cooperation with them, was extremely wary of the information he received from the British. Repeated instances of British openness and candor, though, overcame U.S. distrust sufficiently to enable the cooperative relationship between the two countries.

6. Be mindful of the target's concerns about the relationship

Despite all their efforts, the British were still prone to miscalculation about how some of their overtures would be perceived by the Americans. A case in point was Godfrey's visit, during which he attempted to get the U.S. to adopt some of the same interdepartmental intelligence organizations that the British possessed. Godfrey's efforts demonstrated a lack of understanding of the U.S. political landscape and American sensitivities about being told by the British how to run their affairs. Godfrey should have borne in mind the experience the British had in forming its own Joint Intelligence Committee. Despite their greater tradition of interdepartmental intelligence coordination and the pressures of actual conflict, they still had problems making the JIC function effectively even a year into the war. Either naiveté or hubris on their part had led them to expect the American intelligence system to adopt a similar system on their recommendation. Had the British been more sensitive to U.S. perceptions of them and the American concerns about the relationship, they would have realized that recommendations on how to organize the U.S. war effort were bound to generate significant resentment. Waiting until the relationship was more mature and on surer footing would have been more appropriate and effective, given the level of U.S. concern over British attempts to dominate their partnership.

Remaining Questions

Although numerous studies address this period, as documented in the bibliography attached to this work, some questions remain to be explored.

1. Why did BGEN Strong make the offer to share SIGINT information with the British during the Standardization of Arms Talks? At what level was this decision authorized? Why was the Navy not informed of the offer before it was made?

2. How influential were Kirk's attaché reports? While it is obvious that the DNI, RADM Anderson, and the CNO, ADM Stark, read Kirk's reports, there are indications that the Secretary of the Navy and the President read them as well. Although we do know that Kirk's reputation was overwhelmingly positive, how much credibility was given to his attaché reporting concerning Great Britain's chances for survival after the fall of France?

3. What was the exact nature of the relationship between William Stephenson's BSC and the U.S. Navy? Did ONI realize that information it was receiving from the FBI originated with the BSC? When did ONI begin cooperating with the BSC and what were their impressions of the organization? Other than Stephenson's connections with Donovan and Knox and the cooperation between ONI and the BSC in counterintelligence efforts, did the BSC attempt to influence Navy Department policies through any other overt or covert mechanisms?

4. What was the full extent of information exchanged through the Joint Bailey Committee mechanism? Which side benefited more from the exchange of information through that mechanism—the British or the Americans?

Conclusion

Evidence clearly shows that the "special relationship" that developed between the U.S. and the UK during World War II had its antecedents in the interwar period and came about as a result of aggressive tactics on the part of the British to obtain that relationship as part of their overall effort to secure U.S. support for their war effort. While not necessarily a well-coordinated effort, it was persistent and occurred on numerous levels, particularly in the period from the start of World War II through the Pearl Harbor attack. The British were able to capitalize on a period of shared national interest with the U.S. to secure their objectives and overcome the inherent tensions in their relationship with America. The intelligence-sharing relationship survived the war and has been unprecedented in both its longevity and its depth. This study bears lessons for present-day and future policymakers who may wish to foster intelligence-sharing arrangements with states that have had historically inimical or competitive ties with America.

GLOSSARY

ABC-1	American-British-Canadian Staff Talks
ALUSNA London	American Legation, U.S. Naval Attaché, London
BGEN	Brigadier General
BSC	British Security Coordination
CAPT	Captain, Navy
CDR	Commander
COI	Coordinator of Information (U.S.)
COMINT	Communications Intelligence
CSS	Central Security Service (British)
DCI	Director, Central Intelligence (U.S.)
DNC	Director of Naval Communication (U.S.)
DNI	Director of Naval Intelligence (U.S. and British)
FECB	Far East Combined Bureau (British)
FBI	Federal Bureau of Investigation
GC&CS	Government Code and Cipher School (British); also known as Bletchley Park
HF/DF	High Frequency/Direction Finding
HUMINT	Human Intelligence
IC	Intelligence Community
JIC	Joint Intelligence Committee (British)
JPS	Joint Planning Staff
JSM	Joint Staff Mission (British)
MAGIC	Decrypted PURPLE Intercepts
MGEN	Major General

MI5	Security Service (British); Domestic Counterintelligence
MID	Military Intelligence Division (both U.S. and British)
NA	National Archives
NHC	Naval Historical Center, Washington Navy Yard
NID	Naval Intelligence Division (British)
NSA	National Security Agency (U.S.)
OIC	Operational Intelligence Center (British)
ONI	Office of Naval Intelligence
OPINTEL	Operational Intelligence
OSS	Office of Strategic Services (U.S.)
PCO	Passport Control Office (British)
PURPLE	Japanese Diplomatic Code
RADM	Rear Admiral
SIGINT	Signals Intelligence
SIS	Secret Intelligence Service; also known as MI6 (British) Overseas Clandestine HUMINT Service
SOE	Special Operations Executive (British)
Station CAST	U.S. SIGINT Station at Corregidor in the Philippines
VADM	Vice Admiral

APPENDIX A

A NOTE ON SOURCES

Archival sources for this paper were primarily found in three repositories in the Washington DC area—The Naval Historical Center at the Washington Navy Yard; The National Archives, both the College Park, Maryland and Washington, DC branches; and the Special Collections section at the United States Naval Academy Library. Of these, the Naval Historical Center (NHC) had the most extensive collection of relevant material. The most significant set of records was the *Papers of Alan Goodrich Kirk*. Kirk, in his role as the U.S. Naval Attaché in London, was in a pivotal position during a critical juncture in U.S.-UK relations. His detailed reports to his superior, DNI RADM Walter S. Anderson, provide the clearest indication of England's attempts to court U.S. support for their war effort and also illustrate the underlying tensions in the U.S.-UK relationship that worked against cooperation. The NHC also contains *The Reminiscences of Alan Goodrich Kirk*, which are part of the Columbia University Oral History Archives and contain many of VADM Kirk's observations and recollections from the period under review. His reminiscences are very consistent with the official records found in his papers, and the personal insights he provides give added depth and clarity to some of the issues identified in his official reporting from this period.

Another valuable source at the NHC is the *Papers of ADM Harold Stark*. In addition to the Plan Dog Memo, ADM Stark's papers contain numerous pieces of personal and official correspondence from this period that clearly illuminate the thinking of this key decisionmaker. Other important sources at the NHC include the *Papers of Royal E. Ingersoll, The Reminiscences of RADM Royal E. Ingersoll, and the Papers of Frank Knox*. Ingersoll's papers and reminiscences provide amplifying details on the mission he undertook to London in early 1938, while Knox's papers contain the text of his speeches that illustrate his thinking concerning support for the British war effort.

At The National Archives (NA), the operational archives of the Navy contain the correspondence files of the Office of Naval Intelligence (ONI). These correspondence files, which are housed at the Washington, DC branch of the NA, proved helpful in illuminating some aspects of naval intelligence cooperation and technical exchange forums such as the Tizard Mission and the Standardization of Arms Talks. The College Park, MD branch of the NA contains a complete set of the ALUSNA London correspondence concerning exchange of information with the Joint Bailey Committee. Finding other relevant source material at the NA was a difficult process for two reasons. First, the NA staff is still engaged in cataloging material recently transferred from the NHC. Unlike the collections the NA has held for an extensive period, such as the ONI correspondence files, there are currently no detailed finding aids developed for the NA's newer acquisitions. Second, records are, for the most part, split along chronological lines at the NA. Materials dated prior to 1940 are housed in the Washington DC branch and records post-1940 are held at the College Park facility. Future researchers are advised to work closely with a naval archivist to ascertain the location, scope, and availability of the records at the NA.

The Naval Academy Library also proved a good source of primary source material. In particular, the Library houses a special collections room which contains reminiscences of individuals, such as RADM Arthur H. McCollum, who conducted the intelligence exchange visit to the UK in the late summer of 1941. In addition to providing information on this visit, McCollum's reminiscences are full of useful insights concerning the U.S. naval establishment during this period. Another significant source of information held at the Naval Academy is *Strategic Planning in the U.S. Navy: Its Evolution and Execution 1891-1945*, a microfilm resource which contains many of the primary-source documents related to such significant events as the Ingersoll Mission in 1938, the Standardization of Arms Talks in 1940, and the American-British-Canadian (ABC-1) Staff Talks of 1941. The Library also houses bound collections of relevant primary-source material related to foreign policy from the Office of the President, Franklin Delano Roosevelt. In addition to documents related to U.S.-UK relations, these bound collections contain correspondence between Roosevelt and his Secretary of the Navy, Frank Knox, and with the CNO during this period, ADM Stark, all of which is helpful for understanding the ongoing dialogue between Roosevelt and his advisors. These papers demonstrate how Roosevelt was committed to helping Great Britain for U.S. national security reasons, but they also reveal how large a factor domestic political constraints and the desire to retain equality with Great Britain were in his decisionmaking. Additionally, the Library contains a complete collection of the State Department's *Foreign Relations of the United States*. These collections were instrumental for understanding some of the points of tension between the two countries, such as colonialism, while also illuminating the factors that led to the strategic rapprochement between the two countries in the mid-1930s.

Finally, *The London Journal of General Raymond E. Lee, 1940-1941*, edited by James Leutze and also found at the Naval Academy Library, can easily be overlooked, but is an outstanding primary source for understanding this period. Lee was the Army attaché in London at the same time as Kirk, and his views of the situation offer a useful contrast with those provided by Kirk and others.

APPENDIX B

MAJOR EVENTS IN U.S.-UK INTELLIGENCE COOPERATION

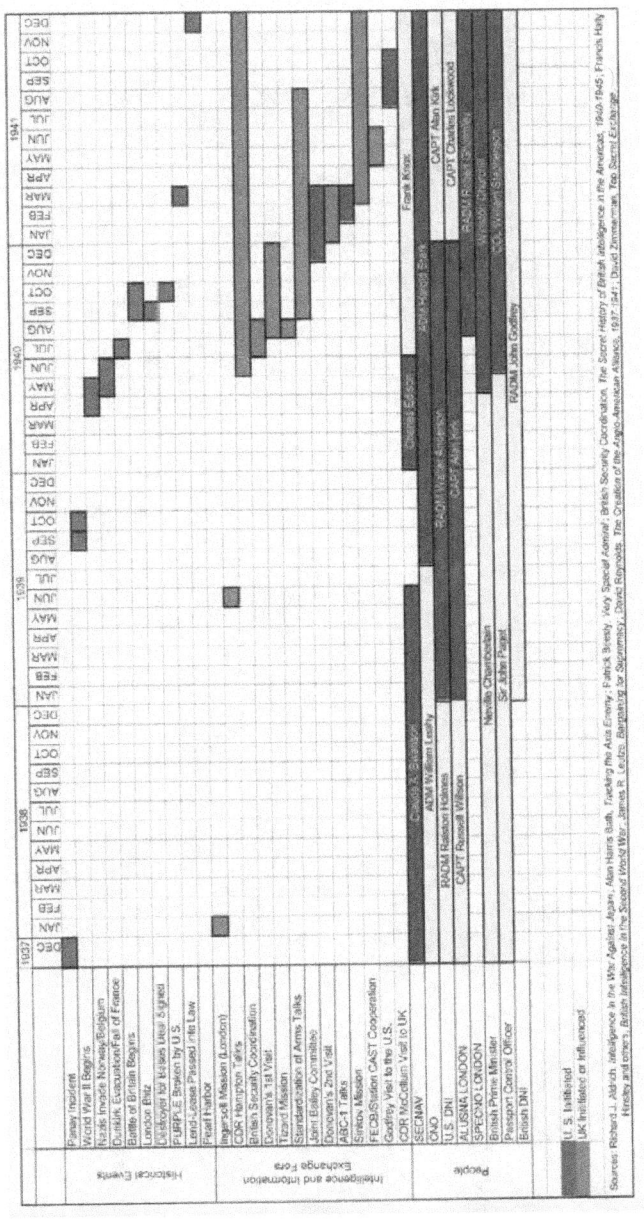

BIBLIOGRAPHY

Archival Sources

Department of the Navy. Secretary of the Navy, Confidential Correspondence. Record Group 80. National Archives Building, Washington DC.

_____. Division of Naval Intelligence General Correspondence, 1929-1942. Record Group 38. National Archives Building, Washington, DC.

_____. Records of the Naval Operating Forces. U.S. Naval Forces Europe Subject File: From Bailey Committee thru Bolero. Record Group 313. Stack Area 370, Row 30, Compartment 1, Shelf 05, NN3-38-90-3. National Archives Building, College Park Maryland.

Papers of Alan G. Kirk. Operational Archives Branch, Naval Historical Center, Washington, DC.

Papers of Frank Knox. Operational Archives Branch, Naval Historical Center, Washington, DC..

Papers of Harold R. Stark. Operational Archives Branch, Naval Historical Center, Washington, DC.

Published Primary Sources

British Security Coordination. *The Secret History of British Intelligence in the Americas, 1940-1945*. New York: Fromm International, 1999.

Columbia University. *The Reminiscences of Royal E. Ingersoll*. New York: Oral History Research Office, 1965. Operational Archives, Naval Historical Center, Washington, DC.

_____. *The Reminiscences of Alan G. Kirk*. New York: Oral History Research Office, 1962. Operational Archives, Naval Historical Center, Washington, DC.

Department of State. *Foreign Relations of the United States, 1920*. Washington, DC: GPO, 1936.

_____. *Foreign Relations of the United States, 1921*. Washington, DC: GPO, 1936.

_____. *Foreign Relations of the United States 1922*. Washington, DC: GPO, 1936.

_____. *Foreign Relations of the United States 1934*. Washington, DC: GPO, 1951.

_____. *Foreign Relations of the United States 1940*. Washington, DC: GPO, 1958.

Franklin D. Roosevelt and Foreign Affairs, December 1937-February 1938. Ed. Donald B. Schewe. New York: Garland Publishing, Inc., 1979.

Franklin D. Roosevelt and Foreign Affairs, January 1939-August 1939. Ed. by Donald B. Schewe. New York: Garland Publishing, Inc., 1979.

Leutze, James R. *The London Journal of General Raymond E. Lee, 1940-1941*. Boston, MA: Little, Brown, and Company, 1971.

McCollum, Arthur H. *Reminiscences of Rear Admiral Arthur H. McCollum, U.S. Navy, Retired*. Vol. 1. United States Naval Academy Library Special Collections.

Strategic Planning in the U.S. Navy: Its Evolution and Execution 1891-1945 in the U.S. Naval Academy Library microfilm collection. Wilmington, DE: Scholarly Resources, Inc., 1979.

Secondary Sources

Albion, Robert Greenhalgh. *Makers of Naval Policy, 1798-1947*. Ed. Rowena Reed. Annapolis, MD: Naval Institute Press, 1980.

Aldrich, Richard J. *Intelligence and the War Against Japan: Britain, America, and the Politics of Secret Service*. Cambridge: Cambridge University Press, 2000.

American-British-Canadian Intelligence Relations 1939-2000. Ed. David Stafford and Rhodri Jeffreys-Jones. Portland, OR: Frank Cass Publishers, 2000.

Baer, George W. "U.S. Naval Strategy 1890-1945." *Naval War College Review 44*, no. 1, sequence 333 (Winter 1991): 6-35.

Bath, Alan Harris. *Tracking the Axis Enemy: The Triumph of Anglo-American Naval Intelligence*. Lawrence, KS: University Press of Kansas, 1998.

Beesly, Patrick. *Very Special Admiral: The Life of Admiral J. H. Godfrey*, CB. London: Hammish Hamilton, Ltd, 1980.

_____. *Very Special Intelligence: The Story of the Admiralty's Operational Intelligence Center 1939-1945*. Garden City, NY: Doubleday & Company, INC., 1977.

Best, Antony. *Britain, Japan, and Pearl Harbor: Avoiding War in East Asia, 1936-1941*. New York: Routledge, 1995.

Bray, Jeffrey K. *Ultra in the Atlantic*. Laguna Hills, CA: Aegean Park Press, 1994.

Charmley, John. *Churchill's Grand Alliance*. New York: Harcourt Brace & Company, 1995.

Coles, Michael. "Ernest King and the British Pacific Fleet: The Conference at Quebec, 1944 ('Octagon')." *The Journal of Military History 25*, no. 1 (January 2001): 105-129.

Doron, Gideon. "The Vagaries of Intelligence Sharing: The Political Imbalance." *International Journal of Intelligence and Counterintelligence* 6, no. 1 (Summer 1993): 135-146.

Dorwart, Jeffery M. *Office of Naval Intelligence: The Birth of America's First Intelligence Agency 1865-1918*. Annapolis, MD: Naval Institute Press, 1979.

_____. *Conflict of Duty: The U.S. Navy's Intelligence Dilemma, 1919-1945*. Annapolis, MD: Naval Institute Press, 1983

Erskine, Ralph. "Churchill and the Start of the Ultra-Magic Deals." *International Journal of Intelligence and Counterintelligence* 10, no. 1 (Spring 1997): 57-74.

Ford, Corey. *Donovan of OSS*. Boston, MA: Little, Brown, and Company, 1970.

Hinsley, Francis Hally, and others. *British Intelligence in the Second World War: Its Influence on Strategy and Operations*. London: Her Majesty's Stationery Office, 1979.

Jakub, Jay. *Spies and Saboteurs: Anglo-American Collaboration and Rivalry in Human Intelligence Collection and Special Operation,1940-45*. New York: St. Martin's Press, Inc., 1999.

Knowing Your Friends: Intelligence Inside Alliances and Coalitions from 1914 to the Cold War. Ed. Martin S. Alexander. Portland, OR: Frank Cass Publishers, 1998.

Leedy, Paul D., and Jeanne Ellis Ormrod. *Practical Research: Planning and Design,* 7th ed. Upper Saddle River, NJ: Prentice-Hall, Inc., 2001.

Leutze, James R. "Technology and Bargaining in Anglo-American Naval Relations: 1938-1946." *Proceedings* 103, no.6, sequence 892 (June 1977): 49-61.

_____. "The Secret of the Churchill-Roosevelt Correspondence: September 1939-May 1940." *Journal of Contemporary History* 10, no. 3 (July 1975): 465-491.

_____. *Bargaining for Supremacy: Anglo-American Naval Collaboration, 1937-1941.* Chapel Hill, NC: The University of North Carolina Press, 1977.

Lewin, Ronald. *Ultra Goes to War.* New York: McGraw-Hill Book Company, 1978.

MacLachlan, Donald. *Room 39: A Study in Naval Intelligence.* New York: Atehneum, 1968.

Mahl, Thomas. *Desperate Deception: British Covert Operations in the United States, 1939-1944.* Washington, DC: Brassey's Inc., 1998.

Morison, Samuel E. *The Battle of the Atlantic, September 1939-May 1943.* Vol. 1 of *The History of United States Naval Operations in World War II.* Boston, MA: Little, Brown, and Company, 1947.

_____. *The Rising Sun in the Pacific, 1931-April 1942.* Vol. 3 of *The History of United States Naval Operations in World War II.* Boston, MA: Little, Brown, and Company, 1948.

Muir, Malcolm Jr., "Rearming in a Vacuum: United States Navy Intelligence and the Japanese Capital Ship Threat, 1936-1945." *The Journal of Military History* 54, no. 4 (October 1990): 473-485.

Niblack, Albert P., CAPT, USN. "Forms of government in relation to their efficiency for war." *Proceedings* 46 (September 1920): 1402-1430.

Packard, Wyman H. *A Century of Naval Intelligence.* Washington, DC: GPO, 1996.

Persico, Joseph E. *Roosevelt's Secret War.* New York: Random House, 2001.

Pratt, Lawrence. "Anglo-American Naval Conversations." *International Affairs* 47 (October 1972): 745-763.

Reynolds, David. *The Creation of the Anglo-American Alliance 1937-41: A Study in Competitive Co-operation.* Chapel Hill, NC: The University of North Carolina Press, 1982.

Richelson, Jeffrey T. "The Calculus of Intelligence Cooperation." *International Journal of Intelligence and Counterintelligence* 4, no. 3 (Fall 1990): 307-323.

Schlesinger, Arthur M. *The Coming of the New Deal*. Vol. 2 of *The Age of Roosevelt*. Boston, MA: Houghton Mifflin Company, 1959.

Smith, Bradley F. *The Ultra-Magic Deals: And the Most Secret Special Relationship, 1940-1946*. Novato, CA: Presidio Press, 1993.

_____. "Admiral Godfrey's Mission to America, June/July 1941." *Intelligence and National Security* 1, no. 3 (September, 1986): 441-450.

Spector, Ronald H. *Listening to the Enemy: Key Documents on the Role of Communications Intelligence in the War with Japan*. Wilmington, DE: Scholarly Resources, Inc., 1988.

Stripp, Alan. *Codebreaker in the Far East*. London: Frank Cass Publishers, 1989.

U.S. War Department. History Project, Strategic Services Unit, *War Report of the OSS (Office of Strategic Services)*. New York: Walker and Company, 1976.

Weiss, Steve. *Allies in Conflict: Anglo-American Strategic Negotiations, 1938-44*. New York: St. Martin's Press, Inc., 2001.

The White House. "Joint Statement Between U.S. and India." 9 November 2001. *The White House*. URL:<http://www.whitehouse.gov/news/releases/2001/11/20011109-10.html>. Accessed 16 November 2003.

The White House. "Press Briefing by National Security Advisor Dr. Condoleezza Rice on the President's Trip to Europe and Russia." *The White House*. URL:<http:// www.whitehouse.gov/news/ releases/2002/05/20020520-9.html >. Accessed 16 November 2003.

Winton, John. *Ultra in the Pacific: How Breaking the Japanese Codes and Cyphers Affected Naval Operations Against Japan, 1941-45*. Annapolis, MD: Naval Institute Press, 1993.

Wirtz, James J. "Constraints on Intelligence Collaboration: The Domestic Dimension." *International Journal of Intelligence and Counterintelligence* 6, no. 1 (Spring 1993): 85-99.

Worth, Roland H. *Secret Allies in the Pacific: Covert Intelligence and Code Breaking Cooperation Between the United States, Great Britain, and Other Nations Prior to the Attack on Pearl Harbor*. Jefferson, NC: McFarland, 2001.

Zacharias, Ellis M., CAPT, USN. *Secret Missions: The Story of an Intelligence Officer.* New York: G. P. Putnam's Sons, 1946.

Zimmerman, David. *Top Secret Exchange: The Tizard Mission and the Scientific War.* Montreal: McGill-Queen's University Press, 1996.

ABOUT THE AUTHOR

CDR Florence is a career naval officer who served tours in engineering, operations, and combat systems as a Surface Warfare Officer before transitioning to Naval Intelligence. In his intelligence tours, he has served as the intelligence officer for an electronic reconnaissance squadron in Japan, as an Amphibious Squadron Intelligence Officer, and most recently in the Joint Staff J2 (Intelligence Directorate) at the Pentagon. He is now Head of the Current Readiness, Systems, and Fleet Support Department at U.S. Fleet Forces Command in Norfolk, Virginia. He graduated from the U.S. Naval Academy in 1988 with B.S. degrees in History and English, and from the Joint Military Intelligence College with a Master's of Science of Strategic Intelligence in 2003. His interest in exploring the pre-WWII UK/U.S. intelligence relationship stemmed from his love of military and diplomatic history and his desire to look for lessons from the past that could be applied to today's national security challenges.

INDEX

D

Davis, Norman 28-30
Denniston, Commander Alistair 13, 83, 90
Destroyers-for-Bases Deal 39, 61-62, 73
Director of Naval Communications, OP-20-G 7, 9, 82
Director of Naval Intelligence (DNI) 5-6, 9, 15, 45, 65-66, 78, 88
Donovan, Colonel William "Wild Bill" 60-63, 69, 71, 89, 96

E

Eden, Anthony 31-32
Embick, Major General S. D. 78
Emmons, Major General C. 71
Enigma 82-83, 90

F

Far East Combined Bureau (FECB) 13, 86-87
Federal Bureau of Investigation (FBI) 2, 6, 58-59
Fleming, Commander Ian 89
Friedman, William 82-83, 91

G

Ghormley, Rear Admiral Robert L. 35-36, 40, 71-82, 97
Godfrey, Rear Admiral John 43-44, 47-49, 51-56, 63, 68, 82, 86, 87-92, 96-97
Government Code & Cypher Service (GC&CS) -
  Bletchley Park 10-11, 13, 83-84, 90

H

Hall, Rear Admiral Sir Reginald "Blinker" 8, 17
Halsey, Admiral William "Bull" 46
Hampton, Commander T.C., mission to U.S. 35-36, 72
Hart, Admiral T.C. 40, 77
Hill, Archibald Vivian (A. V.) 63, 68
Hinsley, Francis 1, 10, 13
Holmes, Rear Admiral Ralston 6
Hoover, J. Edgar 58
Hull, Cordell 28-31
Human Intelligence (HUMINT) 2, 7, 10, 12, 60-61, 88

N

National Defense Research Council (NDRC) 66, 68
Naval Arms Limitation 18, 25-26, 30
Naval Intelligence Division (NID) 8, 12
Naval Research Laboratory 65
Naval War College 19
Niblack, Captain Albert P. 15
Norden bombsight 34, 66

O

Office of Naval Intelligence (ONI) 2-10, 13, 59-60, 76, 88, 92
Office of Strategic Services 4, 62
Operational Intelligence (OPINTEL) 8, 12, 32, 52-53, 81, 90-92
ORANGE (Japan) 19

P

Paget, Sir James 58
Panay Incident 31, 35
"Plan Dog" memorandum 40, 70, 77-78
Political Warfare Executive 10, 62-63
Pound, Admiral Sir Dudley 64, 68, 74, 92
Propaganda 53, 58-59
"Purple" 3, 82-83

Q

Quackenbush, Lieutenant Robert S. 81
Quid pro quo, as policy 27, 34, 45-47, 50-52, 57-58, 63-68, 95-96

R

RAINBOW FIVE 41
Roosevelt, Franklin
    Delano 3, 28, 31, 37-39, 41, 50, 55, 58, 60-62, 69-70, 73, 79, 82, 85, 90, 93

S

San Remo Agreement, 1920 21
Secret Intelligence Service (SIS - MI6) 10-11, 13, 58-60, 62, 87-88
Security 4, 59
Security Service (MI5) 10, 58